Spiritual Companions

For
Kay and Malcolm Hare,
who appreciate
and buy
good books

SPIRITUAL
COMPANIONS

AN INTRODUCTION
TO THE
CHRISTIAN CLASSICS

PETER TOON

BAKER BOOK HOUSE
Grand Rapids, Michigan 49516

Contents

Introduction

Recently, it was my privilege to edit *A Guidebook to the Spiritual Life* (Marshall-Pickering, 1988). In this Dr Arthur Skevington Wood takes the reader on a guided tour of Great Britain, stopping here and there at the home or place of work associated with the writer of an important book on the spiritual life of the Christian. For example, in East Anglia, where I was a rector for seven years, he visits a small town, Lavenham, to recall that it was here that William Gurnall, while rector there, wrote his *A Christian in Complete Armour*; then, crossing over the border from Suffolk to Norfolk he goes to Norwich to see the cell where Mother Julian, the anchoress, recorded the *Revelations* given to her by our Lord.

In his tour Dr Skevington Wood makes the point that as Christians we are united to fellow Christians both through space and through time. By an extension of the Church's influence through space we can benefit today from the writings of Christians in all parts of the world (e.g. I have been deeply moved by the insights of Hans Urs Von Balthasar and his friend Adrienne Von Speyr); and by an extension in time we can draw on the wisdom of the centuries to assist us in our pilgrimage today. As I hope the contents of this book will show, there is a vast storehouse of heavenly and practical wisdom at our disposal in the spiritual classics, ready for us to digest and allow to mould us after the pattern of Jesus Christ. Thomas à Kempis spoke for thousands when he remarked that the devout find their delight in a quiet corner (even also on a commuter train!) with a little book (or even perhaps a large book!). Hence the title, *Spiritual Companions*.

1

However, for Christians there is no book to replace the Bible; no other literature can ever be of equal worth to the sacred Scriptures. All other books, however deeply pervaded by a genuinely Christian spirit, must assume a secondary and a supplementary role. For only in the Old and New Testaments is found the authoritative record of God's saving, redeeming and reconciling work for humankind. It is from these holy books that the Church reads in public worship and develops her teaching on faith and morality. They provide the content of God's self-revelation in the Law, the Prophets and distinctively in and through Jesus, the Christ. They are unique and irreplaceable.

Why, then, it may be asked, should we bother with other books about faith, morals and spirituality? If a Christian has only a small amount of time to read then she or he surely ought to read only the Bible, and perhaps, only the Gospels. However, if it is the case that there is sufficient time for reading alongside and with the sacred Scriptures, then what could be better than the reading of what we may call the classics of spirituality produced in the Church over the centuries since the death of the apostles. These books have a particular way of sending their readers back to the Bible with more insight and commitment to benefit from hearing it read aloud or meditating upon it personally. Further, the reading of these classics produces a desire and a tendency (as meditating upon Scripture also especially does) to seek God – 'My soul thirsts for the living God'.

John Wesley prayed that he would be a man of one book (*homo unius libri*). The Preface to his *Forty-Four Sermons* has an eloquent paragraph on this topic as he explains his approach to the Bible and the way he meditates upon it. However, though his ambition was to be a 'man of one book', he did enthusiastically read other books, and with great profit. He edited and published *The Christian Library* in fifty volumes between 1750 and 1756 containing edited selections from a wide variety of writers on the Christian life, some of whom are included in this volume. His aim was to make the Methodists into people of one book – paradoxically by profiting from the reading of a number of carefully chosen books.

What is a classic?

I would say that a classic is a book which is, and has been, recognised in large parts of the one, holy, catholic and apostolic Church as an important, formative influence towards holiness and Christian maturity. Further, it can be read over and over again and nearly always with profit.

There are a few books which virtually all informed Christians from the various Christian traditions (Greek Orthodox, Roman Catholic, Protestant) would certainly regard as classics: and then there are many other books which would be listed as classics but not everyone would provide the same list. The more a person has read of the treasures of the differing Christian traditions of spirituality the more varied her or his list will be. For there are classics in each of the major streams of the Christian tradition and, we may add, there are a few classics in those minor streams which do not necessarily flow into the major ones.

Why this selection?

To choose one hundred classics of spirituality was not easy. My choice is of course wholly personal and is based upon my wide reading and extensive travelling over the last thirty or more years. I have been the guest of many seminaries, colleges, monasteries, churches and organisations in Russia, Greece, Italy, Switzerland, France, Germany, Israel, Sweden, Canada, USA, Latin America, Australasia and Asia. From these contacts I have both learned much and also extensively deepened my appreciation of spirituality in traditions other than the Church of England where I serve an ordained pastor.

Certain definitions and criteria were before me as I made the selection, which perhaps will be better understood if I list them.

1. By 'spirituality' I mean the work of the Holy Spirit as the Spirit of Christ within the whole Church, and in each Christian believer, bringing a deep and sustained desire for holiness, maturity, perfection, godliness, prayerfulness, faithfulness, and compassion.(See my *What is Spirituality? And is it for me?* D.L.T., 1989).

2. By 'spirituality' I mean 'Trinitarian spirituality', a form of worship, discipleship and service which is offered to God the Father through God the Son in the Holy Spirit. A classic is a book whose contents positively affirm the Gloria: 'Glory be to the Father and to the Son and to the Holy Spirit, as it was in the beginning, is now and ever shall be, world without end. Amen.' In the light of this definition I have left out books by Jacob Boehme and well-known Quaker writers, for I am not sure about their Trinitarianism.

3. I restricted the choice to texts available in English translation and published at least once this century in Britain or North America. However, most have seen several or many printings.

4. I chose only those texts which do not require particular theological knowledge or training in order to be understood. Though in some cases interest needs to be matched with effort, the texts are open to all. Thus I have not included certain writers who have been enormously influential but who are very difficult to follow – e.g. Pseudo-Dionysius, Meister Eckhart and Evagrius.

5. I decided not to include any books written after 1939, the year of my birth! More importantly this year was the year when World War II broke out, bringing vast changes to our world. It is very difficult to judge which modern books truly

deserve the title of a classic. I can think of several which probably do deserve the title but I judge it best not to mention them here. Perhaps there is need for another book to do honour to these.

6. I made the attempt to be genuinely ecumenical, including books from the period we call the patristic age, from the Greek Church of the East and the Latin Church of the West, from the Churches of the Reformation and from the Third World. Finding books from the latter category has been difficult but I have included two. (Happily, there has been a tremendous acceleration of writings from the churches of Africa and Asia since 1939.)

Finally, perhaps I need to say that I could have included another twenty or other books. I found it extremely difficult to decide which ones to leave out and I doubt if I shall be ever absolutely satisfied with the final choice. The wealth of material left to us by men and women who walked closely with God and who were gifted to express the truth of their experiences, is totally overwhelming.

Do the writers disagree?

When I survey the underlying theologies in the one hundred books I see that there are basically three different approaches to understanding the way to be holy and perfect before God. The Greek approach is known as deification – the imparting of the divine life into the soul from Christ (who is the God-Man and Mediator) through the Holy Spirit who is the Third Person of the Trinity. Thus communion and union with God is the goal of salvation and is possible for human beings as they seek to lose their dependence upon the world and the flesh and are transfigured by the light of God's grace (see e.g. pp. 89–90).

The medieval Western approach, continued in Roman

Catholic thought, is that of the three ways – the purifying/ cleansing of sin; the enlightening/illuminating of the mind; and the becoming one with God by grace. These are not logical steps but three necessary experiences (not once for all but repeatable) of the soul in the movement from being self-centred and sinful to being holy, righteous and pure, delighting in God's presence. At all times God looks for cooperation in this work from the baptized Christian (see e.g. pp. 203–204).

The Protestant approach has centred on the relationship of justification and sanctification. Justification is the act of God in placing a believing sinner in a right relationship with himself through forgiving his sins and adopting him into his family of forgiven children. On the basis of this there is the process of sanctification wherein a person is made holy through the indwelling Spirit's power and by the response of faithfulness, obedience and trust (see e.g. pp. 57–58).

There are theological books from Roman Catholics criticising the Greek approach and from Greek Orthodox writers tearing apart the Roman Catholic approach. Then there are books by Protestants complaining about both the Greek Orthodox and Roman Catholic approaches. Christians have always loved to disagree! Yet the amazing fact is that each tradition has, by the grace of God, produced saints. It would seem that where the heart of man is set upon seeking the face of God in Jesus Christ, the Mediator, then one's preferred spiritual tradition simply becomes a context for meditation, contemplation, practical holiness and profound communion with God. As they gaze upon God in the light of Jesus what the saints see is the same infinite, eternal deity, who is a Trinity of Love. Parties and sects will indeed one day fall away. Perhaps it also needs to be added that each of the three traditions is capable of producing genuine Christians.

I am not saying that theology does not matter. What I am saying is that communion and union and fellowship with God, the Holy Trinity, does not come about merely by having a correct or viable theology. Unless the heart is set on fire with the love of God and unless the will is dedicated to seeking him and obeying him, then the best and most correct doctrines in Christendom will never alone create holiness.

Perhaps I need to add that the best way to read classics of the spiritual life is with the intention of sincerely seeking to implement what one learns from them in one's life with God. This kind of reading will call for our response in greater faith and love. If we read without a willingness to hear and respond, we run the danger of hardening our hearts.

A reader's guide

The books are introduced not chronologically but alphabetically according to the author's name. My aim in introducing each book has been to say a little about the writer, the content, and what is special about this book. One or more shorter or longer quotations is included. The general aim is to encourage the reader to look for the book, examine it and hopefully read it through for himself or herself: perhaps one a month for the next eight years!

Some will be disappointed because I have not attempted to list all the various editions of each book. A public or university library has the means of helping you track down particular editions of any book; further, a good bookshop will be able to tell you whether a book is in print or not. You may find that a nineteenth-century edition is preferable to a modern one.You may even be able in some cases to read the original in French or German or Spanish. Generally, I have listed the editions which are most readily available, in order to encourage their further reading. Several publishers, you will discover, produce series of classics from Christian writers. For example, *The Classics of Western Spirituality* from SPCK and Paulist Press; *Hodder Christian Classics* from Hodder and Stoughton and *Orchard Books* from Burns & Oats. It is well worth browsing through the publishers' catalogues. An endless and infinitely varied feast awaits the hungry reader; this collection is offered as a modest *hors d'oeuvre*.

The Vicarage,
Staindrop,
Co Durham.

Peter Toon
The Feast of St Augustine, 28 August 1989

1

A Sure Guide to Heaven

JOSEPH ALLEINE
(1634–1668)

Alleine as a pastor, writer, and a godly and learned man is an excellent example of an English Puritan clergyman who became a Nonconformist minister. He was ordained in 1655 but ejected in 1662, along with nearly 2,000 others, because he could not in conscience accept the new order in the Church under Charles II. He was imprisoned for preaching the Gospel outside the parish system and, not recovering from his confinements, died at the age of thirty-four, when he was contemplating missionary work in Wales or abroad.

However, his most influential book, through which breathes his holiness and evangelistic zeal, was not published until 1672, four years after his death. It became a best-seller and has had great influence in leading people to Christ. This century it has been reprinted at least six times. Strangely it had in the seventeenth and eighteenth centuries three titles: *An Alarm (or A Call) to the Unconverted* and *A Sure Guide to Heaven*. It may claim to be the finest short exposition in the English language of what believing in the Lord Jesus Christ and turning from sin to God the Father really means. Though the illustrations are dated, the message rings as true now as it did in the seventeenth century.

Here is how Alleine writing in the preface saw his task:

Some of you do not know what I mean by conversion, and

in vain shall I attempt to persuade you to that which you do not understand. Therefore, for your sakes, I will show what conversion is.

Others cherish secret hopes of mercy, though they continue as they are. For them I must show the necessity of conversion.

Others are likely to harden themselves with a vain conceit that they are converted already. To them I must show the marks of the unconverted.

Others, because they feel no harm, fear none, and so sleep as upon the top of a mast. To them I shall show the misery of the unconverted.

Others sit still, because they do not see the way of escape. To them I shall show the means of conversion.

And finally for the quickening of all, I shall close with the motives to conversion.

The beginning of true, Christian spirituality is conversion to God, the Father of our Lord Jesus Christ. This book contains a view of what genuine conversion – turning from a self-centred life to a Christ-centred one – entails. As such it still speaks eloquently to those who have ears to hear and eyes to see. It has the merit of being short, clear and compelling! It is a mistake to write it off – as some have done – as merely an example of Puritan zeal. It can speak for God to persons of any background and religious tradition, concerning their relationship to him in time and eternity.

2

Private Devotions

LANCELOT ANDREWES
(1555–1626)

Andrewes was famous as a preacher at St Paul's Cathedral, London, and his *Ninety-Six Sermons* remains a classic of Anglican preaching. He held high office in the Church of England under both Elizabeth I and James I, ending his career as Bishop of Winchester. As a Bible translator, he was primarily responsible for Genesis to Deuteronomy and for I Kings to II Chronicles in the Authorised (King James) Version of 1611. As a theologian he was one of those who helped to create a distinctively Anglican Protestant theology.

He was also a man of deep personal piety and spirituality. Throughout his ministry he collected for his own personal use prayers and devotions from Holy Scripture and ancient books of prayers and liturgies. Parts of the collection were published in an English translation in 1648 by Richard Drake under the title *A Manual of the Private Devotions and Meditations of Lancelot Andrewes*. The first comprehensive edition of the manuscript left by Andrewes was produced by the Clarendon Press in 1675 (edited by John Lampshire) and entitled *Peces Privatae, Graece & Latine*. Since then it has appeared in various translations but the best are those based on the edition of Canon F.E. Brightman which first appeared in 1903.

As the title indicates it is a book of actual meditations and prayers, and suggestions or outlines for meditations and prayers. Andrewes' deep regard and affection for Scripture will

11

not be seen to mould all his devotional thought. His prayers are often built on a framework of biblical sentences and phrases. Here, the material is primarily Scriptural but with additions from ancient books of liturgy and devotion. All is woven together in a distinctively Anglican style. Here, as an example, is a short piece on prayer:

If not seven times like David; (Ps 119:164)
   yet three times like Daniel? (Dan 6:10)
If not, like Solomon, at length; (1 Kgs 8:22ff)
   yet, like the Publican, shortly? (Lk 18:13)
If not for a whole night, like Christ; (Lk 6:12)
   yet for a single hour? (Matt 26:40)
If not on the ground, if not in ashes; (Mk 14:35;Dan 9:3)
   yet not in bed? (Song of S. 3:1)

Here is another on fasting:

If not in sackcloth; (Jonah 3:8)
   yet not in purple and fine linen? (Lk 16:19)
If not wholly from all; (2 Sam 3:35)
   yet from dainties? (Dan 1:8)

This book is a collection for anyone who wishes to deepen or vary their daily period of meditative prayer. On the surface it may not appear exciting; only in the use of it can one experience the depth of biblical knowledge and confidence which has gone into its making.

3

Book of Visions

ANGELA OF FOLIGNO
(c.1248–1309)

Angela came from a wealthy family and spent virtually all her life in Foligno in Umbria. She married, had children and lived a typical worldly life, enjoying her affluence. Becoming an admirer of the Franciscan way, she became a Franciscan tertiary* but was not truly converted until she had seen her mother, husband and children all die. Thus her gradual journey towards the Franciscan ideal was long and painful; but having finally embraced the life of poverty she began to feel the joy and comfort which came from knowing God in her heart.

In her openness to God she received various visions and enjoyed a particularly deep sense of the love of God both for her and within herself. Her most profound experience of the presence and love of God occurred when she made a pilgrimage from Foligno to Assisi. Here in the chapel dedicated to God, the Holy Trinity, she had a deep, mystical sense of God as Father, Son and Holy Spirit, pouring his love into her soul.

She dictated her visions to her uncle, Arnoldo, a Franciscan friar, and he wrote them down. They are both mystical in spirit

---

*A tertiary is a member of the Third Order of the Roman Catholic Church, a religious society of lay-persons which is affiliated to a religious order and follows its rules in a modified form.

and often self-critical; their major themes are the 'Uncreated eternal trinitarian love of God' and the image of God within the human soul. They present and offer what Angela calls 'Divine Consolation'.

Of prayer she wrote:

> It is through prayer and in prayer that we find God. There are various kinds of prayer but in these three kinds alone is God to be found. The first is corporal, the second mental, and the third, supernatural. (Then, after describing the first two she continues . . .) Supernatural prayer is that during which the soul is so exalted by this knowledge, or meditation, or fullness of God that it is uplifted above its own nature and understands more of God than it otherwise could naturally understand. And understanding, it knows; but that which it knows it cannot explain, because all that it perceives and feels is above its own nature . . .

For Angela the path to deeper communion with God is through the ascetic life of mortifying sin and via the path of both vocal and mental prayer. There are no short cuts to the gracious felt presence of the Saviour for God only reveals himself to those whom he has prepared through the means of grace he offers.

It is interesting to note that her writings were valued by both Catholics and Lutherans in the sixteenth and seventeenth centuries. In fact Johann Arndt (see p. 15) quotes from them at length in his *True Christianity* (1606). They have value today also as records of genuine Christian mystical experiences given by God to a laywoman. Thus, Angela's book provides good reading for a retreat, and stimulating reading on prayer.

4

Prayers and Meditations

ANSELM OF CANTERBURY
(1033–1109)

Anselm is famous as a theologian, philosopher and churchman. He was Archbishop of Canterbury from 1093–1109. He wrote an important book on the Atonement of Christ, *Cur Deus Homo*, and advanced the Ontological Argument for the existence of God in his *Proslogion*. (This is the argument that God exists because the concept of 'God' necessitates the existence of such a being.) Like St Augustine before him, Anselm saw in genuine faith (faith in God and in his self-revelation recorded in Scripture) the precondition for the right use of reason both in meditating and in living according to theology. This basic approach is often expressed as *credo ut intelligam* – I believe in order that I may understand.

He wrote his *Prayers and Meditations* in a Latin rhyming prose when he was abbot of Bec in Normandy, before he moved to Canterbury. They were written at the request of others to provide guidance on how to meditate and pray privately outside the regular services of monastery, convent or cathedral. The best modern version is edited by Benedicta Ward.

At first sight the nature of fourteen of the nineteen prayers may be off putting to Protestants for they are addressed not to God or Christ but to Mary, the apostles and saints. However, they turn out to be profound conversations within the 'communion of saints'. All the prayers are to be read slowly for they provide much food for thought and prayer. Then there

15

are three meditations which contain soliloquy (addressing oneself in God's presence) and colloquy (dialogue with God): again they are rich in content and fine examples of theological meditation and thorough self-examination.

Of special interest today is the way Anselm presented what may be called the 'motherhood' of Jesus* in his rôle as the one who by his passion and death brought forth children for the kingdom of God. This teaching appears in his 'Prayer to St Paul'

And you, Jesus, are you not also a mother?
 Are you not the mother, who, like a hen,
 gathers her chickens under her wings?
Truly, Lord, you are a mother;
 for both they who labour
 and they who are brought forth
 are accepted by you.
You have died more than they, that they may labour to bear.
 It is by your death that they have been born,
 for if you had not been in labour,
  you could not have borne death;
and if you had not died, you would not have brought forth.
 For, longing to bear sons into life,
  you tasted of death,
 and by dying you begot them . . .

---

*It is important to note that while he describes Christ as a Mother he does not address God as Mother.

16

5

True Christianity

JOHANN ARNDT
(1555–1621)

Arndt, a Lutheran pastor in Germany, has been aptly described as 'a prophet of interior Protestantism'. The majority of his writings are on spirituality and the most famous and useful are *The Four Books on True Christianity* (1605–1610). His attraction for readers from the seventeenth to the twentieth century lies both in his emphasis on the mystical union of the believer with Christ within the Body of Christ, and his incorporation of the insights of late medieval piety into a commitment to the great Lutheran teaching on being given righteousness by faith. In these matters he was the true successor of Luther. In fact, it has been said that he underpins Luther's own vision that being given righteousness by faith alone – far from being opposed to good works – actually causes, releases and reinforces good works in the world, church and home. Thus, if there were no other, here is one solid reason why he ought to be read carefully by modern-day Protestants.

The titles of the four books – *Of Scripture, Of Christ, Of Conscience* and *Of Nature* – hardly do justice to their contents. The first is really all about genuine, real, mind-in-heart, committed Christianity. 'He who wishes to be a true Christian must endeavour to let one see Christ in him, in his love, humility and graciousness, for no-one can be a Christian in whom Christ does not live.' Book Two is about true discipleship inspired by the Spirit of Christ. Introducing this book he wrote these inspired words:

> By the lowliness and humility of our Lord Jesus Christ, we climb up as on a true ladder to heaven into the heart of God, our dear Father, and we rest in his love. In Christ's humanity we must begin and arise into his divinity. There in Christ we see into the heart of our dear Father in heaven, we contemplate God as the highest, eternal, essential, infinite good, as the immeasurable power, as the unfathomable mercy, as the unsearchable wisdom, as the purest holiness, as the unassailable and infinite righteousness, as the sweetest goodness, as the loveliest graciousness, and as the most gracious loveliness, as the kindest blessedness. These are the chief aspects of the contemplative life.

Book Three is for those who are advancing in Christian maturity while Book Four is on the use of God's creation as a means to love, worship and serve God himself.

It is difficult to get a complete English translation of all four books but there are several translations of Book One, which is the most important of the four. The best is that by Peter Erb (1979). For those who want to know how Christian mysticism fits into a Protestant approach to the Bible and also how a life of loving service flows from the gift of righteousness by faith, this is a book to study. However, it is probably best read after Luther himself (see p. 125) has been read.

6

Life of Antony

ATHANASIUS
(296–373)

Athanasius, who became Bishop of Alexandria in Egypt in 328, is justly remembered as the man who fought valiantly to uphold the biblical and orthodox truth that Jesus is really and truly God become Man, the eternal Word become flesh. Thus his short yet powerful treatise *On the Incarnation* is of great importance for Christian orthodoxy.

As a true pastor and teacher, Athanasius was most concerned that people not only believe properly but pray and behave properly also. In the interest of holiness he composed the *Life of Antony* soon after his death in 356. Though written quickly, it was to become one of the most influential writings in Christian history. It has inspired not only the monastic movement but also commitment to the ascetic life by clergy and lay-people alike. He has been seen not only as the monk to be imitated but also as the Christian providing an ideal pattern of the disciplined, ascetic life.

Antony came from a Christian home but felt the call to a deeper communion with God and discipleship of Jesus after hearing the words of Jesus to the rich young man (Matt 19:21). He gave away all his possessions and began the new chapter of his life seeking to live by faith and to pray without ceasing. This meant resisting the temptations of the world, flesh and the devil – and part of the power of Athanasius' narrative is his description of Satanic temptation and the ensuing spiritual battle. Antony held that

'When I am weak, then I am strong' through Christ (2 Cor 12:10).

Eventually Antony sought greater solitude on the mountain of Pispir in an abandoned fort. Yet he was not a solitary. Many people came to him for counselling, prayer, healing, exorcism and teaching. Athanasius shares with his readers some of these stories and Antony's teaching. He also describes the powerful attacks of the devil: for example in section 52 we read:

> Then the devil watched Antony closely and (as David sings in Ps. 35:16; 37:12) gnashed his teeth against him. But Antony was comforted by the Saviour, remaining unaffected by his treacheries and various ploys. He sent beasts against him in the night as he lay sleepless; and nearly all the hyenas in that wilderness, emerging from their dens, surrounded him, and he was trapped in their midst. But as each one opened his mouth and threatened to bite, he, acquainted with the ways of the enemy, said to them all, 'If you have received authority over me, I am prepared to be devoured by you. But if you were sent by demons, waste no time in retreating, for I am a servant of Christ.' When Antony spoke these words they fled, being driven away by the remarks as by a whip.

He was God's physician to Egypt and he died at the ripe old age of 105 years, looking forward to being with his Lord.

7

The Confessions

AUGUSTINE OF HIPPO
(354 – 430)

The *Confessions* are contained in ten books of autobiography which cover Augustine's life from childhood through to his conversion to Christ in AD 387. This book is not only important because it is written by one of the greatest of the theologians of the Christian Church but also because it is a profound insight into the workings of God within a human life. It has been produced in thousands of editions and is, by any reckoning, one of the great books not only of Christian but also of the world's literature.

Written at the request of friends at least ten years after his baptism, it represents not only autobiography but also Augustine's mature reflection upon God's dealings with him and his response to the divine grace, providence and guidance. Its format is that of a dialogue with God as he surveys his past life in conversation with the God who is now his Redeemer and Sanctifier. Thus it begins with these words addressed to his Lord: 'You prompt him to take delight in praising you, because you made us for yourself, and our heart is restless until it finds its rest in you.'

The story begins in North Africa where he was born and tells of his education there, followed by his teaching of rhetoric at Thagaste and Carthage. It continues as he crosses over the sea to Italy, first to Rome and then to Milan. All the time he is searching for truth, God, beauty, meaning and purpose. At

Milan he encounters the great bishop, Ambrose, and is much impressed by his teaching and preaching of Christianity. Then his Christian mother, Monica, arrives from North Africa to be near him. Soon her prayers for her son are answered as he hears one day in a garden a voice saying, 'Pick it up and read it.' He was reading Paul's Epistle to the Romans and so he picked it up and his eyes fell upon chapter 13 verses 13–14, '. . . Clothe yourselves with the Lord Jesus Christ . . .' Christ had found him; he had found Christ. Later he was baptised and began his Christian life. His mother was overjoyed but soon afterwards she died. The narrative part of the autobiography ends with his prayers for Monica.

The autobiographical reflections are in Books 1–9. In Book 10 we have a series of mature reflections. Here is the 27th:

Late I came to know you (O God), Beauty ancient yet new. Late I loved you. But, see, you were within me while I was abroad. There I was seeking you. Deformed though I was, I was rushing upon those beauties of your creation. You were with me but I was not with you. Those beauties kept me far away from you: beauties which would not have existed, were they not in you. You cried and called aloud and broke my deafness. You flashed, shone and shattered my blindness. You breathed fragrance, I drew in my breath, and I panted for you. I tasted, I hunger and I thirst. You touched me and I burned for your peace.

God is truly Light, Life and Beauty for Augustine.

8

On the Trinity

AUGUSTINE OF HIPPO
(354–430)

In the *Confessions*, Augustine had much to say about the soul's ascent to God and how God has graciously come to us in order that we can humbly respond to his call to enter into communion with him. In this very important book, Augustine presents what may be called a Trinitarian mystical theology in the format of a profound theological meditation. It is not as difficult to read as are most of the attempts by scholars to summarise it: the reading of it shows how theology can be prayerful meditation, holy thinking and devout attention to what God has said and done in his self-revelation.

In the first seven books of *On the Trinity* Augustine attempts to establish from Scripture what God has revealed of himself as a Trinity, One God who is Father, Son and Holy Spirit. Then in the next eight books he seeks to understand what he believes and to show how the human soul can truly contemplate this Trinitarian God in whom he believes. Thus the second half of this theological meditation is on the ascent of the soul to God. And the key to this understanding of this divine ascent is that the soul is created in the image and likeness of God. As such it reflects a trinity of mind, love and knowledge 'when the mind knows itself and loves itself'.

Augustine does not ask that unbelievers should first try to understand the Holy Trinity and then believe. They should begin by 'believing what the Scriptures contain concerning the supreme Trinity that is God' and then 'let them go on by prayer and inquiry and right living to the pursuit of understanding'. As for himself, the Bishop of Hippo confesses in the last book: 'I dare not claim to have said anything worthy of the ineffable greatness of the supreme Trinity' and thus decides to bring his book to its ending with adoration and petition in the form of a written prayer. Part of it reads as follows:

. . . I have sought Thee, and have desired to see with my understanding what I believed; and I have argued and laboured much. O Lord my God, hearken to me, lest through weariness I be unwilling to seek Thee; 'but that I may always ardently seek Thy face' (Ps 105:4). Do Thou give strength to seek, who hast made me to find Thee, and hast given me the hope of finding Thee more and more. My strength and infirmity are in thy sight; preserve the one and heal the other. My knowledge and my ignorance are in Thy sight; where Thou has opened to me, receive me as I enter; where Thou hast closed, open to me as I knock. May I remember Thee, understand Thee, love Thee. Increase these things in me until Thou renewest me wholly . . .

O Lord, the one God, God the Trinity, whatever I have said in these books that is of Thine, may they acknowledge who are Thine; if anything of my own, may it be pardoned both by Thee and by those who are Thine. Amen.

It is a book which provides perfect reading for Trinity Sunday and the season of Trinity.

9
Holy Wisdom
AUGUSTINE BAKER
(1575–1641)

Born at Abergavenny in Wales, Augustine Baker trained as a lawyer. He converted to the Roman Catholic Church and then became a Benedictine monk. He helped revive the English Benedictine Congregation (now at Ampleforth) but also spent nine years at Cambrai as spiritual director to the English Benedictine nuns. It was here that he wrote many little treatises on prayer.

These treatises were collected together by Serenus Cressy and published after Baker's death with the title, *Sancta Sophia* (1657). In editions since 1890 the title has been *Holy Wisdom*. This book has been, and remains, a great favourite especially with Catholics who are drawn to contemplative prayer. Its special merits are its careful and clear exposition of the different states of prayer; its well-argued justification for the contemplative life as being a right use of time and service of God; its defence of what was called 'private inspiration' (inner promptings of the Holy Spirit); and its description of making acts of the will as a preparation for communion with God. Though the style is (for our times) heavy the content is stimulating.

Baker has much to teach those Christians who go on retreats to learn the art of contemplative prayer. He sets out with clarity the way of prayer which holy women and men have taken, and how they may be followed in their desire and determination to know God through the experience of being at one with him, and to become mature within the love of God.

To find good quotes from this well argued and logical book is not easy. Here is what he says in the very last chapter on the arrival at the state of perfection in prayer:

By reason of this habitation and absolute dominion of the Holy Spirit in the souls of the perfect (who have neglected, forgotten, and lost themselves to the end that God alone may live in them, whom they contemplate in the absolute obscurity of faith) hence it is that some mystic writers do call this perfect union the UNION OF NOTHING WITH NOTHING, that is, the union of the soul, which is nowhere corporally, that has no image nor affections to creatures in her; yes, that has lost the free disposal of her own faculties, acting by a portion of the spirit above all the faculties, and according to the actual touches of the Divine Spirit, and apprehending God with an exclusion of all conceptions and apprehensions; thus it is that the soul, being nowhere corporally or sensibly, is everywhere spiritually and immediately united to God, this infinite Nothing. The soul is now so elated in spirit that she seems to be all spirit and, as it were, separated from the body. Here she comes to a feeling; indeed, of her not-being and, by consequence, of the not-being of creatures.

This sounds complicated but it is an attempt to describe that which is beyond description – the union of the soul with God.

The best edition of *Holy Wisdom* is that of Dom Gerard Sitwell, which appeared in 1972.

10

The Long Rules

BASIL THE GREAT
(330–379)

Basil is one of the honoured names in the Greek Orthodox Church – thus 'the Great'. He is remembered for his contribution to doctrine (see his *On the Holy Spirit*), liturgy (there is a *Liturgy of St Basil* still in use) and the organisation of monasticism both in the East and West. In character he was eloquent, learned and statesmanlike, and known as a holy man. He forsook the attractions of the world for the life of a hermit by the river Iris near Neo-Caesarea in 358. Here he was joined by his friend, Gregory of Nazianzen, also called 'the theologian'. They developed a monastic establishment on enlightened principles. Eventually the monastery was surrounded by hospitals and hostels for the poor and sick. Here Basil wrote his *Long Rules*, a guide to the nature of monastic life, before he was called into the defence of orthodoxy and the office of Bishop of Caesarea. The *Long Rules* became the basic text, after the New Testament, for the organisation of the monastic life in the East and they inspired Benedict of Nursia (see p. 31) when he wrote his *Rule for Monasteries*.

The *Long Rules* contains a preface followed by the answers to fifty-five questions, put to Basil by his disciples. They do not seem to be in any particular order and some material is repeated. However, in virtually all answers, there is some valuable insight or teaching on personal or community holiness. Though intended for monks much of what he has

27

to say has an immediate relevance to all Christians – for example, loving God and loving one's neighbour in the love of God, the imitation of Christ as the goal of Christianity and the relation of work and prayer.

The seventh answer deals with the superiority of the community life (monastery) over the solitary (isolated) life by listing the advantages of the one over the other. For example:

> For wherewith shall a man show humility, if he has no-one in comparison with whom to show himself humble? Wherewith shall he show compassion, when he is cut off from the communion of the many? How can he practise himself in long-suffering when there is none to withstand his wishes? If a man says he finds the teaching of the divine Scriptures sufficient to correct his character, he makes himself like a man who learns the theory of building but never practises the art, or who is taught the theory of working in metals but prefers not to put his teaching into practice . . . For, behold, the Lord Jesus, because of the greatness of his love for men, was not content with teaching the word only, but in order to give us accurately and clearly a pattern of humility in the perfection of love, he girded himself and washed the feet of his disciples in person. Whose feet will you wash? For whom will you care? In comparison with whom will you be last if you live by yourself? . . .

The *Long Rules* is found in the *Ascetical Works* of Basil.

11

The Saints' Everlasting Rest

RICHARD BAXTER
(1615–1691)

Baxter is perhaps the best known of all the puritan and Nonconformist pastors and writers of the seventeenth century. He enjoyed a most fruitful ministry in Kidderminster (1641–1660); and, at the restoration of the Monarchy, after refusing the bishopric of Hereford, he became a tireless and formidable defender of Nonconformists and Nonconformity. He wrote many books (e.g. *The Reformed Pastor* and *An Alarm to the Unconverted*) and some hymns (e.g. 'Ye holy angels bright . . .'). His autobiography entitled *Reliquiae Baxterianae* (1696) makes for fascinating reading.

The Saints' Everlasting Rest (1650) has often been called a devotional classic. It is a long book and has therefore often appeared in shortened form. The 'rest' is that of Hebrews 4:9, 'there remains a rest for the people of God', which is heaven, at whose centre is the exalted Lord Jesus Christ. Baxter describes this heavenly rest with great eloquence and warmth. The scriptural exposition is thorough and moving. The final part of the book is really a book itself on how to meditate upon Scripture and how, in particular, to meditate upon Christ in glory in heaven. Puritans saw meditating as that means of grace which makes all other means of grace effective: they saw meditating upon heaven (to become truly heavenly-minded) as the highest form of meditation. Baxter is a very clear exponent of these principles; and, for him, to be truly heavenly-

minded is the only way to be truly useful on earth!
Here is an example of his style of meditation:

'Rest!' How sweet the sound! It is a melody in my ears. It lies as a reviving cordial at my heart, and from thence sends forth lively spirits, which beat through all the pulses of my soul. Rest – not as the stone that rests on the earth, nor as the flesh shall rest in the grave, nor such a rest as the carnal world desires. O blessed rest! – when we 'rest not day and night saying, Holy, holy, holy, Lord God almighty!'(Rev. 4:8) When we shall rest from sin but not from worship; from suffering and sorrow but not from joy! O blessed day! When I shall rest with God! When I shall rest in the bosom of my Lord! When I shall rest in knowing, loving, rejoicing, and praising! When my perfect soul and body shall together perfectly enjoy the most perfect God! When God, who is love itself, shall perfectly love me, and rest in his love to me, as I shall rest in my love to him; and rejoice over me with joy: and joy over me with singing, as I shall rejoice in him.

Perhaps in days when contemporary spirituality has little to say about the looking forward to heaven and the developing of heavenly-mindedness this book (often published in *The Practical Works of Richard Baxter*) has a message for us. (See also my *Longing for Heaven*, Macmillan, New York, 1989, which was inspired by *The Saints' Everlasting Rest*).

12

Rule for Monasteries

BENEDICT OF NURSIA
(c.480–550)

Little is known about Benedict. He came from Nursia in Tuscany, and being disgusted with the decadent culture of his time, he set off on a journey to find life in and with God. Eventually he settled on Monte Cassino, on the road between Rome and Naples, and founded a monastery. Here, making extensive use of existing materials, he composed the *Rule* for which he is famous as the 'Patriarch of Western monasticism'.

Thousands of lives have been spiritually formed since the sixth century by this *Rule* and it continues to be the context and guide for the lives in community of many today. It has the appearance of a matter-of-fact document; this is because it is not just spiritual teaching or only a personal code. It is also the structure for a Christ-centred society and thus it has to be realistic about the capabilities and weaknesses of human nature – even when it is Christian and being sanctified!

At the centre of everything is the true 'work of God', the worship of God by the community, the loving God for his own sake because he is truly lovable. Here is what Benedict wrote about the chanting of the psalms in the daily services of worship:

> We believe that God is present everywhere, and that the eyes of the Lord are in every place, keeping watch on the good and the bad (Prov 15:3); but most of all should we believe

this without any shadow of doubt, when we are engaged in the work of God. We should therefore be always mindful of the prophet's words, 'Serve the Lord with fear' (Ps 2:11). And again, 'Sing wisely' (Ps 46:8). And yet again, 'In the sight of the angels I will sing to you' (Ps 137:2). We must therefore consider how we should behave in the sight of the Divine Majesty and his angels, and as we sing our psalms let us see to it that our mind is in harmony with our voice.

The last sentence contains a most important Christian truth: that worship engages the whole person before the Lord our God.

The final chapter deals with the attitude monks ought to have to each other and much the same may be said of church members!

They should with the greatest patience make allowance for one another's weaknesses, whether physical or moral. They should rival one another in practising obedience. No one should pursue what he thinks advantageous for himself but rather what seems best for another. They should labour with chaste love at the charity of the brotherhood. They should fear God. They should love their Abbot with sincere and humble charity. They should prefer nothing whatever to Christ.

The *Rule* ends with the prayer: 'May God bring us all to life everlasting.'

13

On Loving God

BERNARD OF CLAIRVAUX
(1090–1153)

Bernard was first of all a monk who wanted solitude in which to pray, for his whole life was enveloped in the desire for the love of God. He entered the monastery at Citeaux and went from there three years later to establish the monastery at Clairvaux, which under his direction soon became one of the chief centres of the Cistercian order. Bernard attracted disciples from all over Europe and he was much in demand as a guide and counsellor. His warm sincerity, ascetical life, brilliant and winsome eloquence drew hundreds of recruits to his order. He preached and wrote on the love of God, of God's love for man and of man's love for God; and he became one of the greatest exponents of mystical prayer in the history of the Church (see his *Sermons on the Song of Songs*, p. 35).

The core of his teaching on love is found in the short treatise, *On Loving God*. This expands thoughts he had already expressed in a letter to the monks of the Grande Chartreuse. Love begins, he taught, within God himself who is a Trinity of Love. It is revealed in the eternal Son who became man for us and for our salvation. Human beings made in God's image and likeness, possess, with God's gracious help, the capability to love. And it is of this loving of God and one's neighbour of which he writes.

He based his teaching on learning how to love on the analogy of a growing child. First of all there is the self-love of the infant, apparently thinking only of itself; then there is the loving of those who are nearest because of their caring and the good things that they give; thirdly, there is the loving of others just as they are and for what they are; finally there is the love of self, because of being loved by others.

This model is applied by Bernard to the growth of the soul in the loving of God. He saw each stage as essential.

At first a man loves himself for his own sake; he is flesh and able only to know himself. But when he sees that he cannot subsist of himself, then he begins by faith to seek and love God as necessary for himself; and so in this second stage he loves God not for God's sake but for his own sake . . . However, when he has tasted and seen how sweet the Lord actually is, then he passes to the third stage. Here he loves God for God's sake and not for his own. And there he remains for I doubt whether the fourth stage has ever been fully reached in this life by any man – the stage, that is, wherein a man loves himself only for God's sake.

This is a simple but profound analysis. It is deepened in a beautiful way in the *Sermons on the Song of Songs,* which wait to be read after studying *On Loving God.*

14

Sermons on the Song of Songs

BERNARD OF CLAIRVAUX
(1090–1153)

The *Song of Songs* (meaning the greatest of songs) in the Old Testament can be read either as an inspired portrayal of ideal human love within marriage or it can be read as an exquisite presentation of the mutual love of the Lord God for his covenant people. In Christian teaching – less so now than before 1800 – the Song has been interpreted in terms of both the union of love between Christ and his Church and between Christ and the individual member of the Church. St Bernard is one of the finest, if not the finest, exponent of this moving and beautiful interpretation of this *Song*. His teaching on the love of Christ, the Bridegroom, for his Church (and each individual member) as the Bride, as well as the love of the Bride for the Bridegroom leading to their spiritual union in love and in contemplative prayer is presented in the eighty-six sermons, originally preached to the monks at Clairvaux.

There are passages in virtually every sermon which repay repeated reading. Here is part of Sermon 20:

> Learn, O Christian, from the example of Christ the manner in which you ought to love Christ. Learn to love him tenderly, to love him wisely, to love him with mighty love; tenderly, that you be not enticed away from him; wisely, that you be not deceived and so drawn away; and strongly, that you be not separated from him by any force. Delight yourself

in Christ, who is Wisdom, beyond all else, in order that worldly glory or fleshly pleasures may not withdraw you from him; and let Christ, who is the Truth, enlighten you, so that you may not be led away by the spirit of falsehood and error. That you may not be overcome by adversities, let Christ, who is the Power of God, strengthen you. Let charity render your zeal ardent; let wisdom rule and direct it; let constancy make it enduring. Let it be free from lukewarmness, not timid, nor wanting in discretion.

One of the themes in the sermons is the relationship of the contemplative and active aspects of loving of Christ. In true mystical union with Christ both are fulfilled. 'When you shall see a soul which, having left all, cleaves unto the Word with every thought and desire; lives only for the Word, rules itself according to the Word and becomes fruitful by the Word — which is able to say with St Paul "for me to live is Christ and to die is gain" — then you may have assurance that this soul is a bride wedded to the Word.' From this mystical union there arises spiritual motherhood, which has two aspects — continual meditative prayer and the bringing forth of converts through preaching the Word. Here the contemplative and active are combined. Sermon 85 ends with a moving description of the delight in love of the Bridegroom and Bride.

15

Memoir of Robert Murray McCheyne

A.A. BONAR
(1810–1892)

Andrew and his brothers John and Horatius (the hymnwriter), made a famous trio of Scottish clergymen. They were all friendly with R.M. McCheyne, but it was Andrew who wrote his *Memoir*, first published in 1862.

McCheyne lived only thirty years, from 1813 to 1843. After a brilliant university career in Edinburgh, he was ordained to the charge of St Peter's, Dundee in 1836. Here he gave himself unreservedly to meditation, prayer and study each morning and to parish visiting and meetings for the rest of the day. In a very short time he exercised a tremendous influence on the parish and on the Church in Scotland. He was known as a pastor who walked with God and who had a great zeal for the salvation and care of people both in his own parish and elsewhere. People were amazed that one who had such obvious poetic and academic gifts could be so dedicated a parish minister.

Perhaps he exercised a greater influence after his death for the *Memoir and Remains of Robert Murray McCheyne* were widely read and much appreciated not only in Scotland but in many other places as well. Since Bonar was a close friend he had access to the personal diaries and papers of McCheyne and these he used extensively in the book. There are abundant testimonies, especially from pastors and evangelists, as to the spiritual influence of this book upon them, deepening their commitment to the Lord Jesus. Today, though the mid-nineteenth century style may be off-putting to some, the careful reader of this book must be inspired by the story of this gifted young man who gave his all to his Lord in the service of his parish.

Here is an extract from a paper he wrote solely for himself and found by Bonar:

> I am persuaded that I shall obtain the highest amount of present happiness, I shall do most for God's glory and the good of man, and I shall have the fullest reward in eternity, by maintaining a conscience washed in Christ's blood, by being filled with the Holy Spirit at all times, and by attaining the most entire likeness to Christ in mind, will, and heart, that is possible for a redeemed sinner to attain to in this world. I am persuaded that whenever any one from without, or my own heart from within, at any moment, or in any circumstances contradicts these truths (just stated) then that is the voice of the devil, God's enemy, the enemy of my soul and of all good – the most foolish, wicked and miserable of all creatures . . .

Bonar remarked that 'in McCheyne we have been taught how much one man may do who will only press farther into the presence of his God, and handle more skilfully the unsearchable riches of Christ, and speak more boldly for God.'

16

The Soul's Journey into God

BONAVENTURE
(1217–1274)

This was written soon after Bonaventure's election in 1257 as
minister-general of the Franciscan Order and a few years before
he wrote his meditation on the life of Christ, *The Tree of Life*,
and his official *Life of St Francis*. All three are classics but *The
Soul's Journey* is considered his masterpiece.

The physical universe and the human soul are seen as
mirrors revealing God and thereby functioning as ladders
leading to God via the humanity of Jesus, Incarnate Son. There
is an important link between the Franciscan attitude to the
natural world as sacramentally revealing God, and the
Franciscan devotion to Jesus Christ as the fullness of this
revelation. The Christ we meet here is the mystical Christ who
as the Crucified One is the gateway into mystical
consciousness. (For his teaching on the historical Jesus we have
to turn to *The Tree of Life*.) Here, using the Song of Songs, Jesus
is also presented as the Bridegroom united to the believing soul
in the embrace of love.

Bonaventure was inspired to write this book after meditating
upon the vision of St Francis of the six-winged Seraph at the
same place where St Francis saw the vision and received the
stigmata. His symbolic interpretation of the vision provides the
framework of the journey of the soul to God, where mystical
ecstasy awaits. After considering or contemplating God's
reflection in the physical world, through the five senses, and

via his image upon our souls first in their sinful and then in their renewed states, the journey moves on to the meditating upon God, first as Being (the Divine Unity) and then as the Good (the Holy Trinity). The latter contemplative experience of gazing upon Christ fills the soul with wonder and amazement and leads it on to the final stage of mystical ecstasy. At this stage all intellectual activities have been left behind and the soul's affective powers are lost in the loving and adoring of God.

Of the final stage of mystical ecstasy he wrote:

But if you wish to know how these things come about, ask grace not instruction, desire not understanding, the groaning of prayer not diligent reading, the Spouse not the teacher, God not man, darkness not clarity, not light but fire that totally inflames and carries us into God by ecstatic unctions and burning affections.

This fulfils what he wrote in the Prologue: 'I invite the reader to the groans of prayer through Christ crucified . . . so that he will not believe that reading is sufficient without unction, speculation without devotion, investigation without wonder, observation without joy, work without piety, knowledge without love, and understanding without humility.'

17

The Tree of Life

BONAVENTURE
(1217–1274)

Meditating upon the historical Jesus, particularly on his humility, passion and crucifixion is an important element in medieval piety. Francis of Assisi sought to imitate Jesus in his poverty and suffering: therefore there is a strong element of devotion to the humanity of the Son of God in Franciscan spirituality.

The *Tree of Life* is a meditation which involves applying the senses to an imagined scene from the Gospels in order to evoke appropriate emotions varying from love to anguish. The reader is invited to picture in his mind a tree whose roots are watered by an ever-flowing fountain that becomes a great and living river with four channels to water the garden of the entire Church. From the trunk of this tree there are growing twelve branches adorned with leaves, flowers and fruit. The leaves are medicine to prevent and cure sickness, the flowers attract the desires of men by their sweet perfume, and the fruit is there always to satisfy with its attractive taste. 'This is the fruit that took its origin from the Virgin's womb and reached its savoury maturity on the tree of the cross . . .'

While this fruit is one and undivided it nourishes faithful souls according to their needs because of its excellence and power. Its consolations may be reduced to twelve and the tree of life is pictured and offered to the reader's taste under twelve flavours on twelve branches. The twelve branches begin with the birth of Jesus and move on through his life, ministry, passion and death to his exaltation and glorification.

Each branch calls for meditation, prayer and engagement. For example, at the end of the first there is the soliloquy: 'Now, then, my soul, embrace that divine manger: press your lips upon and kiss the boy's feet. Then in your mind keep the shepherds' watch, marvel at the assembling of the host of angels, join in the heavenly melody, singing with your voice and heart: "Glory to God in the highest . . ." '

Then, after meditating upon the death of Jesus there is the prayer:

O my God, good Jesus, although I am in every way without merit and unworthy, grant to me, who did not merit to be present at these events in the body, that I may ponder them faithfully in my mind and experience towards you, my God crucified and put to death for me, that feeling of compassion which your innocent mother and the penitent Magdalene experienced at the very hour of your passion.

For those who are used to the modern academic study of the Gospels this book is most refreshing and helpful for, with its guidance, one is able to experience a living encounter with the Lord Jesus, who was crucified but now lives for evermore. Any danger of sentimentalism is avoided if there is a genuine desire to love and serve the Lord.

18

The Life of St Francis

BONAVENTURE
(1217–1274)

St Francis of Assisi is a saint who continues to have many
admirers and whose spirituality (with its involvement in the
natural world) has much to say when we are so concerned with
the right use of nature. This *Life* is decidedly a spiritual not
a historical or biographical classic: that is, it is a portrait of the
spirituality of Francis through the story of his amazing life. The
first four chapters (dealing with early life, conversion and
founding of the Order) and the last three (dealing with his
receiving the stigmata, death and canonization) are
chronological. The core of the book of nine chapters is
organized according to themes and uses material from the life
of St Francis to illustrate them.

First of all, in chapters five to seven the theme is that of
purgation. We are told of the austerity of his life, of his humility
and total submission to God, and of his love of poverty and
how God miraculously supplied his every need.

Then in chapters eight to ten the theme is illumination. Here
we learn of his affectionate piety, of the affection of birds and
animals towards him, the fervour of his charity, his desire to
be a martyr for Jesus and the depth and strength of his prayers
to God.

Finally, in chapters eleven to thirteen the theme is
perfection. We are told of his understanding of sacred
Scripture, his spirit of prophecy, the power of both his

preaching and healing, and finally of his holy stigmata.

Purgation, illumination and perfection (or union) are often called the purgative, illuminative and unitive ways which lead to God and lie at the centre of the medieval portrayal of how the soul moves from sin through conversion to holiness and communion with God. Francis is presented as a model of the Christian way of life: even as he imitated Jesus, so monks and laypeople imitate him.

The affection of creatures for Francis is well known. We are told how when he was staying at a hermitage to observe a fast 'birds of different kinds flew around his cell, with melodious singing and joyful movements, as if rejoicing at his arrival, and seemed to be inviting and enticing the devoted father to stay. When he saw this he said to his companion, ''I see, brother, that it is God's will that we stay here for some time, for our sisters the birds seem so delighted at our presence''.'

For a delightful biography of St Francis read that by G.K. Chesterton (1924), but for a compelling portrayal of Franciscan spirituality read this powerful presentation. In fact, it is good to read Bonaventure's three classics together, perhaps beginning with this *Life*, then moving on to the *Tree of Life* and concluding with *The Soul's Journey*.

19

The Cost of Discipleship

DIETRICH BONHOEFFER
(1906–1945)

Bonhoeffer is remembered as a critic of the Nazi régime and an active member of the resistance movement in Germany during the Second World War. He had chosen to return to Germany and serve the Confessing Church and was for a short time the head of a theological seminary. Eventually he was arrested by the Gestapo, imprisoned at Buchenwald and executed on 9 April 1945 at Flossenburg, on a charge of treason.

His experience of facing up to the evils of Nazi ideology and practice made him read the Bible, meditate and pray with opened eyes and attentive mind, as well as causing him to treat the confessing of Jesus Christ as the most important thing in the whole world. Preaching in 1935 on Psalm 42:2 he said:

Thirst for God. We know the body's thirst when there is no water; we know the thirst of our passion for life and good fortune. Do we know also the soul's thirst for God? A God who is only an ideal can never still this thirst. Our soul thirsts for the living God, the God and Source of all true life. When will God quench our thirst? When will we come to appear before his presence? To be with God is the goal of all life and is itself eternal life. We are in God's presence with Jesus Christ, the crucified. If we have found God's presence here, then we thirst to enjoy it completely in eternity.

His best known work is *Widerstand und Ergebung* (translated as *Letters and Papers from Prison*, 1953); but the work which most clearly conveys his spirituality is *Die Nachfolge* (1937), translated as *The Cost of Discipleship* (1948).

The first part of *The Cost* . . . explores the distinction between (the all too common) cheap and (the all too rare) costly grace in Christendom. While the former justifies sin but not the sinner, the latter involves both the justification of the sinner by God and the commitment by the believer to genuine discipleship of Jesus Christ. It is this costly grace which Bonhoeffer commends, even though he knows it will mean suffering for Jesus.

In his comments on the Sermon on the Mount he emphasises that those who are truly blessed are those who are living, as it were, at the foot of the cross of Jesus. Only from such a position can meekness, humility, poverty, purity and persecution be offered to God as the salt and light of the world. In fact all good works to achieve their purpose of glorifying God in heaven must be done in and with Christ and never for bringing attention to self.

The call to discipleship is also a call to be a messenger for Christ and to participate in the Body of Christ. This new people must be prepared to commend the Gospel in ways which modern people can appreciate and must also be ready to suffer in its serving of humanity today.

20

Heaven on Earth

THOMAS BROOKS
(1608–1680)

What is lacking in the lives of many Christians is an assurance
from God, deep in the heart, that he is their heavenly Father
and that they are truly his adopted children. 'The Spirit testifies
with our spirit', wrote St Paul in Romans 8:16, 'that we are
God's children.'

In all Protestant literature one of the clearest statements and
explanations of Christian assurance is provided by Thomas
Brooks who was a minister of the Congregational Way in
London in the seventeenth century. The title is associated with
the first of ten advantages which accompany the Holy Spirit's
gift of inward assurance of salvation. 'It will bring down heaven
into your bosoms; it will give you a possession of heaven, on
this side of heaven. An assured soul lives in paradise, and
walks in paradise, and works in paradise; and rests in paradise;
he has heaven within him, and heaven about him and heaven
over him; all his language is Heaven, heaven; Glory, glory.'

The other nine advantages which accompany assurance are
that it sweetens life's changes; keeps the heart from desiring
the world; assists communion with God; preserves from
backsliding; produces holy boldness; prepares a man for death;
makes mercies taste like mercies; gives vigour to Christian
service and leads to a soul's enjoyment of Christ. Thus it both
makes the Christian a more effective disciple of the kingdom
of God and at the same time makes the discipleship the more

enjoyable, and communion with God in prayer the more immediate.

Brooks begins his book by explaining that while assurance is not the essence of being a Christian it is required in order to be a joyful and victorious Christian:

> To be in a state of true grace is to be miserable no more; it is to be happy for ever. A soul in this state is a soul near and dear to God. It is a soul housed in God. It is a soul safe in everlasting arms. It is a soul fully and eminently interested in all the highest and noblest privileges. The being in a state of grace makes a man's condition happy, safe and sure; but the seeing, the knowing of himself to be in such a state, is that which renders his life sweet and comfortable. The being in a state of grace will yield a man a heaven hereafter; but the seeing of himself in this state will yield him both a heaven here and a heaven hereafter; it will render him doubly blest, blest in heaven and blest in his own conscience.

Of course, this gift of God is only given when a Christian is prepared to receive. Thus Brooks provides not only a full and exciting description of the joy of having Christian assurance but also the general conditions for the receiving of this gift and how it differs from counterfeit assurance and presumption.

21

Pilgrim's Progress

JOHN BUNYAN
(1628–1688)

The *Pilgrim's Progress from this world to that which is to come*
(1678) presents in allegorical or symbolical form what *Grace
Abounding to the Chief of Sinners* declares in narrative form.
It was written in prison where Bunyan had been sent because
he preached the Gospel without proper authorisation. It
quickly became a best-seller and maintained that position
until this century. Though it is often analysed today merely
as fascinating literature, for Bunyan it was the fundamental
story of the hazardous route to salvation, heaven and God
– the route away from the devil, sin and hell. Whatever
its literary merits, it is primarily a spiritual classic, telling
of God and his mercy to sinners who believe in Jesus. It
is an allegory of the Christian life, understood according to
the Calvinist, Protestant tradition: yet it is not confined within
this tradition.

In his journey from the City of Destruction to the Celestial
City the man Christian faces many obstacles. These include
both the obviously hostile such as Apollyon (Satan) and the
subtle (e.g. the threats of the false pilgrims whose doctrine is
misleading and whose homes are 'as empty of religion as the
white of an egg is of savour'). But there can be no compromise
and all he meets is either help or hindrance. In fact 'there is
even a way to hell from the gates of heaven'.

The first chapter begins by recounting a dream:

I dreamed and look! I saw a man clothed with rags. He stood with his face away from his own house, a book in his hand, and a great burden on his back. I looked and I saw him open the book and read it. As he read he wept and trembled. Unable to contain himself, he broke down with a heartbreaking cry, calling out 'What shall I do?'

The last chapter tells what happened at the end of the long pilgrimage made by Christian and Hopeful on the narrow way:

I saw that these two men went in at the gate (of heaven). And behold, as they entered, they were transfigured and garments were put on them that shone like gold. Others met them with harps and crowns which they gave to them. The harps were for praise, the crowns were in token of honour. Then I heard in my dream all the bells in the city rang out again for joy, and the pilgrims were told, 'Come and share the Master's happiness'. I also heard Christian and Hopeful singing aloud and saying, 'To him who sits on the throne and to the Lamb be praise and honour and glory and power for ever and ever!'

One of the great values of this book is that it declares very clearly that the Christian life, though lived on earth, must be directed heavenward to be authentically Christ-centred. For the narrow way leads in only one direction – to Christ in heaven!

22

Grace abounding to the Chief of Sinners

JOHN BUNYAN
(1628–1688)

By his own admission, Bunyan had few equals amongst young men for 'cursing, swearing, lying and blaspheming the name of God'. He was a general repairman of household utensils who, after serving as a soldier under Cromwell in the Civil War (1644–6), married a poor girl whose only dowry was a couple of books – *The Practice of Piety* by Louis Bayly and *The Plain Man's Pathway to Heaven* by John Dent. It was the reading of these (then popular) spiritual books about authentic Christianity which began Bunyan's journey towards conversion to Christ.

However, the entering of the narrow gate into eternal life was a painful process of fear and comfort, depression and elation, of doubt and faith, and of darkness and light. He describes a titanic struggle within his soul between the themes of two scriptural texts – Hebrews 6:4–6 and 2 Corinthians 12:9. The first appeared to offer no hope for those who had tasted God's grace and then fallen away (which he thought he had done), while the second asserted that God's grace is sufficient in all circumstances. The second seemed to triumph; but he still had doubts until the message, 'Your righteousness is in heaven', was impressed upon his soul as a word from God.

Now did my chains fall off my legs indeed; I was loosed from my afflictions and irons; my temptations also fled away; so that from that time those dreadful Scriptures of God (containing warnings) left off to trouble me: now went I also home rejoicing, because of the grace and love of God . . .

He then read 1 Corinthians 1:30 which declares that Christ has, by God's design, become for us wisdom, righteousness, holiness and redemption. Pondering this text caused him to have comforting thoughts about Jesus Christ in heaven.

'Twas glorious to me to see his exaltation, and the worth and prevalency of all his benefits, and that because now I could look from myself to him, and would reckon, that all those graces of God that now were green on me, were yet but like those cracked groats and four-pence-half-pennies that rich men carry in their purses, when their gold is in their trunks at home: Oh! I saw gold was in my trunk at home. In Christ my Lord and Saviour. Now Christ was all; all my righteousness, all my sanctification and all my redemption. Further, the Lord did also lead me into the mystery of the union of the Son of God, that I was joined to him, and that I was flesh of his flesh and bone of his bone . . .

So he came to find a settled peace and assurance in Christ and became a preacher and pastor. He wrote his spiritual autobiography in 1666 to celebrate the salvation of God and how 'great sins draw out great grace'. It is a fascinating and moving account, which also includes his first experience of prison in 1660. Read it before reading *Pilgrim's Progress*.

23

The Rare Jewel of Christian Contentment

JEREMIAH BURROUGHS
(1599–1646)

'I have learned', confessed the apostle Paul, 'in whatsoever state I am, therewith to be content' (Philippians 4:11). The book is an exposition of this verse and thus an explanation and commendation of Christian contentment. This is understood as 'that sweet, inward, quiet, gracious frame of spirit, which freely submits to and delights in God's wise and fatherly disposal in every condition' of life.

A Puritan who believed in and practised the Congregational Way in the 1640s, Burroughs was a peace-loving character who was highly respected by his contemporaries. In commending his book (which is an adaptation of a course of sermons on Phil. 4:11) a group of them wrote in the preface:

The only seat this Jewel is ordained for is the precious tablets of men's hearts in and from which alone the native lustre of it will be made conspicuous. Reader, buy it, set and wear it there, and it shall, as Solomon speaks, 'be life unto thy soul, and grace unto thy neck. Thou shalt not be afraid when thou liest down; yea, thy sleep shall be sweet unto thee: for the Lord will be thy confidence'.

The contents include a full description from Scripture and experience of Christian contentment, the 'great mystery and art by which a Christian arrives at this contentment', how

Christ teaches contentment, the evils of a murmuring spirit, the excuses of a discontented heart and how to attain contentment from God in and through Christ. There is a rich use of Scripture and a great knowledge of the human heart displayed in the book, along with wise advice concerning such disciplines as meditation, prayer, and self-examination.

Burroughs makes it clear that 'a contented heart looks to God's disposal, and submits to God's disposal, that is, he sees the wisdom of God in everything. In his submission he sees God's sovereignty, but what makes him take pleasure is God's wisdom. The Lord knows how to order things better than I. The Lord sees further than I do; I only see things at present but the Lord sees a great while from now.' He explains how it is grace which teaches and enables the believer to accept sorrow and joy together and to find contentment through Christ in that acceptance. Only those whose minds and hearts are enlightened by Christ can appreciate and find contentment in sorrow and joy.

This book has a message to all who earnestly desire to find contentment solely in God, in his grace and wisdom. In a world of many pressures and testings true contentment is certainly a rare jewel. Burroughs found this jewel and displays it attractively, even though the sermonic from is not the most attractive of literary styles.

24

Lives of the Saints

ALBAN BUTLER
(1710–1773)

Butler was a priest of the Roman Catholic Church and after extensive research in Europe he published in 1756–9 his *The Lives of the Fathers, Martyrs and other principal Saints, compiled from . . . original records . . .* They were arranged according to the Church Year which meant that some days had more commemorations than others. Butler's chief aim was to edify and inspire and so he does not always distinguish between fact and fiction. However, his massive work was substantially expanded and revised in the 1920s by H. Thurston S.J. and others, with further minor editing in 1956 and 1981 by Donald Attwater in order to make a four volume edition. This latest edition contains 2,565 entries, an average of seven entries for each day of the year, while Butler's original only had 1,486 entries. It is now usually known by its popular title, *Butler's Lives of the Saints*.

In his original preface in 1756 Butler expressed his aim in these wise words:

The method of forming men to virtue by example is, of all others, the shortest, the most easy, and the best adapted to all circumstances and dispositions. Pride recoils at precepts, but example instructs without usurping the authoritative air of a master; for, by example, a man seems to advise and teach himself. In the lives of the saints we see the most perfect maxims of the Gospel reduced to practice, and the most heroic virtue made the object of our senses, clothed as it were with a body and exhibited to view in most attractive dress . . . Though we cannot imitate all the actions of the saints, we can learn from them to practise humility, patience, and other virtues in a manner suiting our circumstances and state of life; and we can pray that we may receive a share in the benedictions and glory of the saints . . .

In commending the latest reprint of the four-volume edition Cardinal Basil Hume of Westminster said this: 'The heroic men and women described and speculated upon on these pages have bequeathed to us an inspiration that transcends ordinary history. It is not surprising, then, that there should be a demand today for yet another edition of *Butler's Lives*. For this present generation seems to be seeking not the letter which kills, but the spirit which awakens.'

There are, of course, other shorter 'Dictionaries' and 'Lives' of the Saints which are valuable but none can replace Butler's not only as an informative but also as an inspirational source of Christian spirituality.

25

Institutes of the Christian Religion

JOHN CALVIN
(1509–1564)

There are treasures in Calvin which many people miss because mistakenly they think of him as the theologian who majors on the damnation of the reprobate. In fact at the centre of his theology/spirituality lies his teaching on the participation of the Church in the sanctification of Christ or the mystical union between Christ and true believers.

By his atoning death and glorious resurrection, Jesus has become in his human nature the fountain from which we must draw whatever we need for our salvation. In uniting us to himself and making us members of his Body, Christ dwells in us through the Spirit and 'he not only brings himself close to us by an undivided bond of fellowship, but by a wondrous communion grows with us daily more and more into one Body until he becomes altogether one with us'. Calvin insists that this mystical union is the very source of both justification (being placed in a right relationship with God) and sanctification (being made holy in heart, mind and will through the indwelling Spirit's power).

From the human perspective it is faith that is the bond of union between Christ and his people. Faith is certainly what is exercised by the sinner who desires salvation; but, it is also the gift of God, created in the soul by the secret action of the Holy Spirit, as people hear the Gospel. So it is true both to claim that union with Christ is by faith and by the Holy Spirit.

The final edition of the *Institutes* appeared in 1559 towards the end of Calvin's work as chief pastor in the city of Geneva. It became the most influential statement of Protestant theology and at the same time is a literary landmark because it was written in French. Calvin chose to use the language of common speech rather than the vocabulary of academic theologians. Possibly no theological writer in history has so well combined the gifts of biblical explanation, logical and clear thought, literary style and pastoral, moral and spiritual care in one powerfully integrated personality.

The *Institutes* are based on the Apostles' Creed and have four parts: first the knowledge of God the Creator; second the knowledge of God the Redeemer; third, the way we receive the grace of Christ; and fourth the external means or aids by which God invites us into the society of Christ and holds us therein. Here we encounter a pastor and teacher deeply concerned both to instruct and to edify, creatively uniting doctrine and morals, teaching and spirituality, individual and corporate piety, prayer, meditation and action. It is a book which, once you have begun to appreciate it you will come back to over and over again or will go from it to one or another of Calvin's commentaries on the Bible.

26

Conferences

JOHN CASSIAN
(360–435)

Though he was a monk writing for monks, what he has to say
has value for people everywhere. A much travelled man he
shared in his twenty-four 'Conferences' that which he learned
from the monks of Egypt. They are reports of conversations
or conferences from the cells of the monks he visited. They
were very influential upon the development of Western
monasticism, in particular its spirituality; and they are being
read again today with great interest by those who want to
develop a 'spirituality of the desert' or are looking for simple
but effective forms of meditation.

Cassian clearly shows that all the self-discipline, fasting,
meditating, praying without ceasing, and other ascetic and
penitential acts – not to mention the struggle with Satan –
of the monks was aimed at one result – an encounter with
the living God and Father of the Lord Jesus Christ.

To gaze with utterly purified eyes on the divinity is possible
– but only to those who rise above earthly works and
thoughts and who retreat with Him into the high mountain
of solitude. When they are freed from the tumult of worldly
ideas and passions, when they are liberated from the
confused melee of all the vices, when they have reached the
sublime heights of utterly pure faith and of pre-eminent
virtue, the deity makes known to them the glory of Christ's

face and reveals the sight of its splendours to those worthy to look upon it with the clarified eye of the spirit.

There is much information about 'purity of heart' and how to achieve it; often this is via simple illustrations.

In Conference 10 there is very useful advice on how to keep the thought of God always in your mind. The simple way is to keep reciting and thinking about the meaning of a particular verse from the psalms (which was the prayer-book of the monks) – 'Come to my help, O God; Lord, hurry to my rescue' (Ps 70.1).

It carries with it all the feelings of which human nature is capable. It can be adapted to every condition and can be usefully deployed against every temptation. It carries within a cry of help to God in the face of every danger. It expresses the humility of a pious confession . . . This is the voice filled with the ardour of love and of charity. This is the terrified cry of someone who sees the snares of the enemy, the cry of someone besieged day and night and exclaiming that he cannot escape unless his protector comes to the rescue.

The reciting of this scriptural verse is not like that of saying an Eastern mantra: for it is said with the mind in the heart, with meaning and with love. (The idea is much the same as in the later development of the recital of the *Jesus Prayer*.)

27

Purgatory

CATHERINE OF GENOA
(1447–1510)

Caterinetta Fieschi Adorna was by any standards a most remarkable saintly woman. She was a married woman, a contemplative, totally involved in the physical care of the sick and destitute at the hospital, a loyal daughter of holy mother Church and the inspiration to many both in her time and afterwards.

Her conversion, as narrated in her *Vita e Dottrina* and which took place when she was twenty-six and married, occurred in this way:

> As she knelt before her confessor, she received in her heart the wound of the unmeasured Love of God, with so clear a vision of her own misery and her faults, and of the goodness of God, that she almost fell upon the ground. And by these sensations of infinite Love, and of the offences that had been done against this most sweet God, she was so greatly drawn by purifying affection away from the poor things of this world that she was almost beside herself, and for this she cried inwardly with ardent love. 'No more world! no more sin!'

She returned home overcome by this experience and shut herself in the most secluded room she could find. All that she could think about and feel was the love of God, and to her was given an interior vision of Christ bearing the Cross. This served to increase more intensely her sense of both the love of God and her own sinfulness.

Both her treatise on *Purgatory* and her *Spiritual Dialogues* were printed within the *Vita e Dottrina*. Scholars appear to have no doubt now that she did write all of *Purgatory* and at least Part I of the *Spiritual Dialogues*. However, it is her short work on purgatory which is the foundation of her reputation as both a mystic and theologian (her saintliness rests upon her life combining both the contemplative and active aspects).

She saw purgatory as the place where the work of purification of the soul, begun in this world, is completed by God, in preparation for entry into heaven. Purification is by suffering both here and hereafter but it ends in true joy in God's presence. Yet purgatory is none other than the experience of God's love eliminating self-love:

Only once do the souls understand the reason for their purgatory: that moment in which they leave this life. After that moment, that knowledge disappears. Immersed in charity, incapable of deviating from it, they can only will or desire pure love. There is no joy (except that in heaven) to be compared to the joy of souls in purgatory. This joy increases day by day because of the way in which the love of God corresponds to that of the soul, since the impediment to that love is worn away daily. This impediment is the rust of sin. As it is consumed the soul is more and more open to God's love.

Having read *Purgatory* move straight on to her *Spiritual Dialogues.*

28

The Spiritual Dialogues

CATHERINE OF SIENA
(c. 1347–1380)

Catherine was the twenty-fourth of twenty-five children and became a patron saint of Italy; and she is one of two women granted the title of 'Doctor' by the Roman Catholic Church. She was always a laywoman, though she joined the third order of the Dominicans. Her political entanglements are not our concern. She is remembered not only for them but also – and this is our interest – as a woman who enjoyed intimate fellowship and rapture with God and who had a tremendous capacity to express this in words. She was a fine example of the union of the contemplative and active aspects of life especially in the last twelve years of her short life.

The *Dialogues* are conversations between God and Catherine. Here is part of what God said to her concerning Jesus, who is portrayed as a bridge between heaven and earth:

This bridge, my only-begotten Son, has three stairs. Two of them he built on the wood of the most holy cross, and the third even as he tasted the great bitterness of the gall and vinegar they gave him to drink . . . The first stair is the feet, which symbolize the affections. For just as the feet carry the body, the affections carry the soul. My Son's nailed feet are a stair by which you can climb to his side, where you will see revealed his inmost heart. For when the soul has climbed up on the feet of affection and looked with her mind's eye

63

into my Son's opened heart, she begins to feel the love of her own heart in his consummate and unspeakable love . . .

The second stair is the heart where one is filled and overcome with the love of Jesus. The third stair is his mouth where the soul tastes peace – from the war against her sins.

In these visions, for the most part dictated by Catherine when she was in a state of ecstasy, there is a wholesome combination of Truth and Love. In fact, for Catherine God as Holy Trinity is *la prima dolce Verità* (the gentle first Truth), *pazza d'amore* (overflowing with love), and *essa carità* (pure charity). Thus the way to God is both the way of truth and the way of love. This dynamic lies at the centre of her teaching and her life and is expressed in the Prologue of the *Dialogues*:

A soul rises up, restless with a tremendous desire for God's honour and the salvation of souls. She has for some time exercised herself in virtue and has become accustomed to dwelling in the cell of self-knowledge in order to know better God's goodness towards her, since upon knowledge follows love. And, loving, she seeks to pursue truth and clothe herself in it.

In continual humble prayer, grounded in the knowledge of God and of herself, she seeks to be united with God by and in love. Read the *Dialogues* for vivid descriptions of her experiences!

29

Self-Abandonment to Divine Providence

J.-P. DE CAUSSADE S.J.
(1675–1751)

Another title for *L'Abandon à la Providence divine* has been *The Sacrament of the Present Moment*. It did not appear for a century after Caussade's death and was put together from his letters and papers by a fellow Jesuit, P. Ramière, in 1861. The book quickly became a source to which mature Christians can return again and again for help and guidance.

Self-abandonment has a particular meaning and it is not the active renunciation of self-will, self-love and self-interest (which he takes for granted). Rather, it is an acceptance of the will of God for which Mary, mother of Jesus, is the exemplar: for she said (and meant) 'Be it unto me according to your word'. Thus it is abandoning oneself to God's direction, grace and providence – much in the same way as a swimmer may be said to abandon himself to the waves as he allows himself to go in their direction.

What he teaches is at once very simple and very difficult to achieve. It is to accept wholeheartedly and wholemindedly that God is in charge and thus to accept everything that happens to one or comes one's way as sent by God and thus to welcome it for Christ's sake. Further, it is to be so conscious of God's presence that the supernatural life is more real than the natural. 'The presence of God which sanctifies our souls is the indwelling of the Holy Trinity, which is established in the depths of our hearts when they submit to the divine will.' And 'this work of the Holy Spirit is not accomplished by way of our own cleverness or intelligence, or subtlety of mind, but by way of our passive self-abandonment to its reception.'

'The doctrine of pure love can only be learned through the action of God, and not as the result of our activity of mind. God instructs the heart by sufferings and contradictions not by ideas.' The crosses which God sends open to us 'a far surer and swifter path to holiness than extraordinary states and works'. The more one appears to lose with God, the more one gains; the more he deprives us of the natural, the more he gives us of the supernatural. We loved him a little for his gifts; when these are no longer perceptible, we arrive at loving him for himself alone.' This is the way to perfection of love when the soul is wholly abandoned to God.

This is the kind of book that is to be read section by section, stopping for reflection and self-examination all the time. It is easy to read but demanding in application. It is for the wise who wish to become wiser; and it is for the holy who wish to become perfect. 'We must learn to let ourselves go passively under the divine action, allowing the Holy Spirit to act within us, without knowing what he is doing, and even content not to know.'

30

The Rise and Progress of Religion in the Soul

PHILIP DODDRIDGE
(1702–1751)

Based at Northampton where he was both a pastor and the head of a Dissenting Academy for training ministers, Doddridge was one of the most influential Nonconformists of the eighteenth century. Several of his hymns, e.g. 'Hark the glad sound . . .', appear in modern hymnbooks and his book, *The Rise and Progress* (1745) can still be read with much profit. It combines the best of Puritan devotion with an evangelical fervour, and presents Christianity as an exciting yet demanding religion.

As the title indicates the book portrays the nature of repentance and faith leading to conversion, the quality of the Christian life required by the Gospel, the temptations and difficulties of this life, the corporate worship and fellowship of believers, and the way to prepare for a Christian death. At the end of each of the thirty chapters there is a meditation and a prayer. The actual reading of these prayers can prove a great help in the development of one's own prayer life for they cover the whole panorama of the beginnings and continuings of the life of grace.

Here is how he defined the subject of his book: 'Religion, in its most general view, is such a sense of God in the soul, and such a conviction of our obligations to him, and of our dependence upon him, as shall engage us to make it our great care to conduct ourselves in a manner which we have reason to believe will be pleasing to him.' We need to add that God, for Doddridge, is God, the Holy Trinity, and religion is in, with and through Christ to the Father in the power of the Holy Spirit.

While there is clear teaching there is also passionate urging and questioning. For example after describing the renewal of the heart in the love of God, he asked his readers to examine their hearts before God:

Do you find there a reverential fear, and a supreme love and veneration for his incomparable excellencies, a desire after him as the highest Good, and a cordial gratitude towards him as your supreme Benefactor? Can you trust his care? Can you credit his testimony? Do you desire to pay an unreserved obedience to all that he commands, and an humble submission to all the disposals of his providence? Do you design his glory as your noblest end, and make it the great business of your life to approve yourself to him? Is your governing care to imitate him and to serve him in spirit and in truth?

There is the same clear and tender questioning on all topics, which is one of the strengths of the book. The last chapter has the title: 'The Christian honouring God by his dying behaviour' and covers relationships with possession, family and with God in a most reverential manner − a timely message for us today.

31

The Greatest Thing in the World

HENRY DRUMMOND
(1851–1897)

This is the best-known work of the Scottish evangelist and writer, who also wrote the widely-read, *Natural Law in the Spiritual World*. He taught natural science in the Free Church College in Glasgow from 1877, but he was also involved in evangelism and was particularly successful amongst students and the educated. It is said that he could have been a great scientist had he not had such a passion to evangelise.

The Greatest Thing in the World is Love, the love described by St Paul in 1 Corinthians 13. This little book is a meditation on that chapter. Its writing belongs to the maturer years of Drummond's life and it is one of the simplest and yet profoundest expositions of this chapter. He divides what he has to say into three parts – Love contrasted; Love analysed; and Love defended.

First of all, in contrast with eloquence, prophecy, mysteries, faith, sacrifice, martyrdom, love stands out supremely. For without love you have nothing and without love Christianity is not genuine.

In the second place, love has nine basic elements, virtues which can be practised by any person in any place. These are patience, kindness, generosity, humility, courtesy, unselfishness, good temper, guilelessness and sincerity. After a short but penetrating exposition of each of these virtues he commented: 'Now the business of our lives is to have these things fitted into our characters. That is the supreme work to which we need to address ourselves in this world, to learn Love. Is life not full of opportunities for learning Love? Every man and every woman every day has a thousand of them. The world is not a play-ground; it is a school-room. Life is not a holiday but an education. And the one eternal lesson for us all is, how better can we love?' Thus practice is the key, daily practice in the exercise of love.

Thirdly, love never fails. It lasts and it lasts forever. Love will abide because God himself is love. 'To love abundantly is to live abundantly and to love for ever is to live for ever. Hence eternal life is inextricably bound up with love.'

Love itself can never be defined. Light is something more than the sum of its ingredients − a glowing, dazzling, tremulous ether. And love is something more than all its elements − a palpitating, quivering, sensitive, living thing. By synthesis of all the colours men can make whiteness, they cannot make light. By synthesis of the virtues, they cannot make love.

Love is only possible by God's grace for love is an effect, and only as we fulfil the right conditions can we have the effect. 'We love God because he first loved us': the key to it all is in the 'because'. By his love we are enabled to love, insisted Drummond.

32

The Life and Diary of David Brainerd

JONATHAN EDWARDS
(1703–1758)

Brainerd (1718–47) has been described as a candle that burned brilliantly but briefly for the Lord Jesus Christ. He died before he reached thirty but through his diary he influenced thousands and thereby achieved more fame in death than in life. He died in the home of Jonathan Edwards because he was engaged to marry Edwards' daughter. In fact Edwards was so impressed with the faith of Brainerd, expressed both in the way he died and in the Diary he left behind that he decided in 1749 to publish it with his own comments, with the prayer that it would show the right way to success in both the ministry and in missionary work. And it has done just that for over two centuries.

After what can only be described as a profound conversion experience Brainerd became an enthusiast for God – so much so that he was expelled from Yale College because of his intemperate zeal. He studied privately, was licensed to preach and appointed by the Scottish Society for the Propagation of the Gospel as a missionary to the American Indians. He longed for communion with God and spent long hours in prayer both to seek God and to pray for the conversion of the Indians. Here is an entry he made on the Lord's Day, July 22, 1744:

When I waked my soul was burdened with what seemed to be before me. I cried to God before I could get out of my

71

bed; and as soon as I was dressed, I withdrew into the woods to pour out my burdened soul to God, especially for assistance in my great work; for I could scarcely think of anything else. I enjoyed the same freedom and fervency as the last evening; and did with unspeakable freedom give up myself afresh to God, for life or death, for all hardships he would call me to among the heathen; and felt as if nothing could discourage me from this blessed work . . .

However, he records that he had little or no success preaching to the Indians that day and ends the entry: 'I was very weak and weary, and my soul borne down by perplexity; but was mortified to all the world, and was determined still to wait upon God for the conversion of the heathen, though the devil tempted me to the contrary.' Yet he laboured on, travelling over 3,000 miles on horseback in his evangelism, and finding some success in 1745 and 1746 with what was called 'a remarkable work of grace'.

To some the comments of Jonathan Edwards on Brainerd may appear unnecessary or laboured. But they are most valuable for not only was he the greatest of America's theologians and philosophers but also a man of great spiritual insight. However, whether an edition of the book is with or without his editorial comments it is a most valuable book. It combines a great zeal to enjoy and glorify the living God with a tremendous desire to see Indians come to know and love the Lord Jesus. It contains mysticism and missions, holiness and evangelism, sincerity and zeal.

33

The Religious Affections

JONATHAN EDWARDS
(1703–1758)

There is no separation of 'head' and 'heart' in the teaching
of Edwards. He was both an intellectual and spiritual giant,
at home in philosophy, spirituality and as a preacher and
pastor. Under his preaching at Northampton, Massachusetts,
there was revival in 1734–5 and again when George Whitefield
was present in 1740–1. He saw many people converted to
Christ and he experienced and observed much enthusiasm and
zeal in the revivals.

This careful observation and pastoral involvement together
with his profound theological ability went into the writing of
The Religious Affections in which he clearly affirms and describes
the inner reality and spirituality of true religion. He begins the
Preface with these words:

There is no question whatsoever that is of greater importance
to mankind and that it more concerns every individual
person to be well resolved in, than this: What are the
distinguishing qualifications of those who are in favour with
God and entitled to his eternal rewards? Or, which comes
to the same thing, What is the nature of true religion? And
wherein do lie the distinguishing notes of that virtue and
holiness that is acceptable in the sight of God?

Therefore one of his primary tasks is to distinguish carefully between true and counterfeit Christianity or between genuine and false religion. And in this enquiry we are led into deep and moving reflections upon the human soul in its relationship with God in and through Jesus Christ.

It may be surprising to some that such a great thinker as Edwards should locate true Christianity primarily in the 'affections' (dispositions of the mind and heart) or in Edwards' words, 'the more vigorous and sensible exercises of the inclination and will of the soul'. He was convinced that the call to be 'fervent in spirit' and to have 'the power of godliness' meant that the true Christian is to be filled with godly fear, ardent hope, perfect love, hatred of evil, desire for God's presence and glory, joy in the Lord, sorrow for sin, gratitude for mercies, compassion for sinners and zeal for the glory of the Lord.

However, he had often witnessed the exercise of the affections in what seemed to be true religion but which proved to be nothing of the sort. Thus he provides an analysis of the true and the false based upon careful scriptural knowledge and pastoral observations. He consistently maintains that genuine affections have their fruit in Christian practice, the actual keeping of the commandments of the Lord. So it is not surprising, for example, that his analysis has proved very helpful in very recent times in congregations which have experienced what is usually called charismatic renewal.

34

Reminiscences

ELIZABETH OF THE TRINITY
(1880–1906)

Elizabeth Catez was born in Avor, northern France, and died in the Carmel of Dijon at the age of twenty-six, after only five years in the cloister. Her short life was consumed by her desire for union with God in holy love.

She prayed daily:

O Divine Master, let my life be but a continual prayer, that nothing, nothing, will be able to distract me from You, neither my occupations, nor my pleasures, nor my suffering, that I may be absorbed in You. Take all my being, that Elizabeth may disappear, that only Jesus may remain.

And, true to the name she was given on becoming a nun, she gave herself unreservedly to the contemplation of Jesus, Incarnate God through whom we enter into the mystery of the Trinity. 'Prayer is a repose, a relaxation,' she wrote. 'One must come in total simplicity to the One whom one loves, holding oneself near to Him as a small child in its mother's arms, allowing one's heart to go out . . . there is only one occupation for a Carmelite and that is to love and to pray.'

As her illness grew progressively worse, Elizabeth still kept up a large correspondence and insisted on giving retreats and writing for them. These letters and her retreats reveal the depth of her spirituality and personality (and are available in *The*

Complete Works, ed. Conrad de Meester, OCD).

She wrote her 'Prayer to the All-Holy Trinity' on an old sheet of paper and it was found in her papers after her death:

> O my God, Trinity whom I adore, let me entirely forget myself that I may abide in You, still and peaceful as if my soul were already in eternity; let nothing disturb my peace nor separate me from you, O my unchanging God, but that each moment may take me further into the depths of your mystery!
>
> Pacify my soul! Make it your heaven, your beloved home and place of your repose; let me never leave you there alone, but may I be ever attentive, ever alert in my faith, ever adoring and all given up to your creative action . . .

She continues by addressing each Person of the Trinity in turn and ends:

> O my 'Three', my All, my Beatitude, infinite Solitude, Immensity in whom I lose myself, I give myself to you as a prey to be consumed; enclose yourself in me that I may be absorbed in You so as to contemplate in your light the abyss of your Splendour!

This prayer may be said to summarise her spirituality which shines so clearly through her own simple but attractive records of her short but significant life in the Carmel of Dijon.

35

Autobiography

CHARLES G. FINNEY
(1792–1875)

Though he was a lawyer, pastor, teacher, and college president, Finney is particularly remembered as an evangelist. Religious revivals were the central priority of his adult life and his great desire always remained that of getting sinners converted to Jesus and setting them to work for him in preparation for his Second Coming. He was a very important figure in American life in the first half of the nineteenth century.

While his *Lectures on Revivals of Religion* may well be called a classic, his life-story published as *Memoirs* or *An Autobiography* needs to be read first and is itself a classic. The account of his religious conversion on 10th October 1821, is a compelling piece of literature in which he tells how he was called to leave a promising legal career because he was given 'a retainer from the Lord Jesus Christ to plead his cause'.

His turning to Christ was accompanied by a baptism by the Spirit:

No words can express the wonderful love that was shed abroad in my heart. I wept aloud with joy and love; and I do not know but I should say, I literally bellowed out the unutterable gushings of my heart. These waves came over me, and over me, and over me, one after another, until I recollect I cried out, 'I shall die if these waves continue to pass over me'. I said, 'Lord I cannot bear any more;' yet I had no fear of death.

His evangelistic career began soon afterwards in upstate New York, after ordination and some theological training.

Over twenty years later he was still experiencing the baptism of the Spirit. Writing in 1843 in Boston he recalled:

During this winter the Lord gave my soul a fresh baptism of his Spirit. I boarded at the Marlborough Hotel, and my study and bedroom were in one corner of the chapel building. My mind was greatly drawn out in prayer. In Boston I had been favoured uniformly with a great deal of the spirit of prayer; but this winter my mind was exceedingly exercised on the question of personal holiness; and in respect to the state of the church, its want of the power of God; the weakness of the orthodox churches in Boston, the weakness of their faith. The fact that they were making little or no progress in overcoming the errors of that city, greatly affected my mind.

He goes on to tell how he would rise at 4 a.m. and often would pray until 8 a.m. until he took breakfast.

He taught that 'revival presupposes that the church is sunk down in a backslidden state and thus consists in the return of the church from her backslidings and in the conversion of sinners . . . It is nothing else than a new beginning of obedience to God.' This is an informative and stimulating book showing how the active life needs to be supported by much prayer!

36

The Works

FRANCIS OF ASSISI
(1182–1226)

Though much has been written about this popular saint few
of his own writings have survived. Since all are short pieces
it is best to take them together as a unit and read them all in
order to gain an insight into what was in his heart and mind
as he lived his life in poverty and imitation of the Lord Jesus.
Francis was the founder of the Franciscan Order of Friars, the
Poor Clares and an Order of Penance for laypeople (known
today as the Secular Franciscan Order). However, it is the
attractive power of his Christlike life which still draws people
of all kinds into the desire to offer their lives to Jesus.

The *Works* can be divided into (i) Prayers and Praises; (ii) the
Counsels of which there are twenty-eight; (iii) letters of which
there are nine; (iv) his testament, composed when he had
resigned as minister-general of the Franciscan Order, and (v)
the First and Second Rules for the Order.

Included in the Prayers and Praises are such well-loved ones
as 'The Song of Brother Sun and of all Creatures' which speaks
of Sister Moon, Brother Wind, Sister Water, Brother Fire, and
Mother Earth as well as 'our sister bodily Death from whom
no man living may escape'. In the Counsels is this short word
on the theme of bodily mortification:

There are many people who always blame an enemy or a
neighbour whenever they themselves do wrong or suffer

hurt. This is not just, for everyone has his enemy in his own power, that is, his own body, by which he sins. Blessed is the servant who keeps such an enemy constantly under his control, and wisely guards himself against him. For, so long as he does this, no other enemy, visible or invisible, can harm him.

And there are these thoughts on the virtues which banish vices:

Where there is charity and wisdom, there is neither fear nor ignorance. Where there is patience and humility, there is neither anger nor vexation. Where there is poverty with joy, there is neither greed nor avarice. Where there is peace and meditation, there is neither anxiety nor doubt. Where the fear of the Lord stands guard, there the enemy finds no entry. Where there is mercy and moderation, there is neither indulgence nor harshness.

Much of what Francis writes is to be pondered over a long period of time rather than read quickly.

However, it is the quality of his life which gives weight and strength and power to what he writes; thus it is advisable to read a biography of this Saint (e.g. that by G.K. Chesterton) before actually using his writings for spiritual reading and meditation. (See also No. 18 above, *The Life of St Francis* by Bonaventure.)

37

An Introduction to the Devout Life

FRANCIS OF SALES
(1567–1622)

In this book the Roman Catholic bishop of Geneva provided for the educated laity the Christian ideal which others had described for clergy, monks and nuns. Holiness is for everyone and everyone is for holiness, be they housewife, soldier, merchant or farmer. It appeared in 1609 and was almost immediately translated into most European languages.

Francis explains what is true devotion, shows how to meditate and pray, teaches what is purity of heart and how to attain it, explains the nature of true virtue and how to practice it, points out the regular temptations of the devil and how to face them, together with wise words on many other topics.

In his Preface he explained that what he was offering was merely a new arrangement of traditional guidance for the practice of holiness: 'I am not able, neither do I wish, nor ought I to write in this book anything which has not been already published on this topic by my predecessors: they are the same flowers that I present . . . but the bouquet (nosegay) which I have made of them will be different from theirs, because it is arranged in a different manner' – that is, designed for the laity. His arrangement has appealed to thousands in every generation from 1609 to the present day. (I have had the pleasure recently of editing a new English translation especially for Protestants published by Hodder & Stoughton.)

Here is a typical statement from Francis:

One of the worst conditions that a person can be in is to be a scoffer: God hates this vice extremely, and has in the past inflicted strange punishments for it. Nothing is so contrary to charity, and much more to devotion, as contempt and scorn for our neighbour. Now derision and mockery can never be indulged in without this contempt; and therefore it is a very grave sin, so that theologians are right in saying that mockery is the worst sort of offence that we can commit against our neighbour by words, because other offenses are committed with some esteem of him who is offended, but this sin is committed with contempt and scorn.

Apart from the very practical nature of the book, another attractive feature is his use of homely and natural illustrations. He travelled on horseback many miles through the Alps and observed bird, insect, animal and plant life, using his observations to illustrate spiritual and moral truths.

While Francis sought to convert back to Roman Catholicism many who had become Protestants through the Geneva Protestant Reformation led by John Calvin, today − and indeed since the seventeenth century − many Protestants have been much helped in their spirituality by his writing.

38

On the Love of God

FRANCIS OF SALES
(1567–1622)

As he was writing *An Introduction to the Devout Life* in 1608 Francis saw that there was need for another book which would be at once both a sequel to it and more fundamental in character and exalted in purpose. He laboured at this work for the next seven years until *On the Love of God* appeared in 1616.

It is certainly a book for those who are desirous of spiritual maturity and who are prepared to be stretched both mentally and spiritually as they read. It is a work of spiritual genius from the pen of a man whose heart, mind and will were intent on loving God perfectly. It is theology done with the mind-in-the-heart and the whole person enveloped in the love of God. Specifically it was written for Jeanne de Chantal, describing for her the stages of the higher reaches of contemplative prayer in a style which is florid but clear. He teaches the acceptance of everything from the hand of God – a cheerful acceptance of God's providence.

Accepting with Teresa of Avila that contemplation is a higher form of prayer than is meditation he explained:

Meditation is similar to one who smells a pink, rose, rosemary, thyme, hyacinth, and orange blossom separately one after the other. Contemplation is like one who smells water containing perfume made up of all those flowers. In a single sensation, the second man takes in all those odours united together, while the other sensed them as separate and distinct. There is no doubt that this one unique odour which comes from the intermingling of all those scents is more sweet and precious than the scents out of which it is composed, smelled separately one after the other. This is why the divine Spouse esteems it so much when his beloved (the Church and believer) looks at him with but one of her eyes, and when her hair is so well braided that it seems like a single hair (Song of Solomon 4:9). What does it mean to behold the Spouse with but a single eye, except to behold him with one single attentive gaze without multiplying glances? What does it mean to wear this braided hair, unless that her thoughts are not scattered over many different considerations? How happy are those who having thought over all their many motives for loving God, and having reduced their looks to one single glance and all their thoughts to one single conclusion, bring their minds to rest in the unity of contemplation!

St Francis of Assisi had reached this stage when he prayed, 'O God, you are my God and my all'.

The last chapter of the long treatise is entitled, 'Mount Calvary is the true School of Love' and that summarises well one of the author's primary emphases. We love God best from the foot of the Cross as we contemplate God with, in and through the Lord Jesus Christ, crucified and risen. 'O supreme love of the Heart of Jesus, what heart can ever bless you as it ought!'

39

The Heart of Christ in Heaven

THOMAS GOODWIN
(1600–1680)

Committed to the Congregational Way and of a Calvinist persuasion, Goodwin was president of Magdalen College Oxford during the 1650s. His *Works*, which contain both academic and devotional pieces, appeared in five folio volumes soon after his death and have been reprinted in whole or in part many times since then.

One of his most moving devotional pieces, which has proved of great interest to many Catholics who have a devotion to the Sacred Heart of Jesus, first appeared with this title: *The Heart of Christ in Heaven towards sinners on earth. Or, a Treatise demonstrating the gracious disposition and tender affection of Christ in his human nature now in glory, unto his members under all sorts of infirmities, either of sin or misery* (1651). It is better known by the shorter title, *The Heart of Christ in Heaven* and is in Volume IV of the modern edition of the *Works*.

Since Goodwin had written other treatises on the resurrection and ascension of Jesus, his sitting at the right hand of the Father and there interceding for us, he took this foundation for granted in this treatise. In his own words his task was to 'lay open the heart of Christ, as now he is in heaven, sitting at God's right hand and interceding for us; how it is affected and graciously disposed towards sinners on earth that do come to him; how willing to receive them; how ready to entertain them; how tender to pity them in all their infirmities . . .' And in this context to encourage believers heartily to come more boldly 'to the throne of grace unto such a Saviour and High Priest when they shall know how sweetly and tenderly his heart, though he is now in his glory, is inclined towards them'. In other words his heart, in respect of its pity and compassion, remains the same as when he was on earth; he is just as meek, gentle and as easily entreated now as he was then.

This is a typical example of English Puritan spirituality. There is, first of all biblical exposition of what Jesus said just before his death (John 14 – 16) and after his resurrection about his post-ascension life and role on behalf of sinners. This is then extended with reference to the teaching of the apostles and particularly what is said about the present role of Christ in the Epistle to the Hebrews. But the biblical material is never treated merely as interesting ancient teaching: the 'uses' of the doctrines and teaching are noted and thoroughly applied especially to the hearts of believers to encourage them in their pilgrimage towards Christ in heaven. So, even though it is not difficult to understand, this book is not popular reading: it is for those who truly want to know what is the attitude of the ascended Christ in glory to human beings looking for spiritual and moral guidance, for encouragement and consolation in this world.

40

The Life of Moses

GREGORY OF NYSSA
(c.330–395)

Appointed by his brother, Basil the Great, as bishop of the small town of Nyssa about 371, Gregory became first a prominent defender and exponent of Christian trinitarian orthodoxy (in relation to the Council of Constantinope in 381) and then in his final period the theologian of the spiritual life.

The *Life of Moses* is believed to be dated about 391. In it he uses the biblical account of Moses (called in Scripture 'the friend of God', Exod. 33:11) as a parable/allegory of the spiritual ascent which the Christian is called to make. This is the ascent from sinfulness to holiness and from the imperfect to the perfect. The meeting with God or being encountered by God, occurs 'in the cloud'. That is, the meeting is without the aid of created vision since God is totally invisible and incomprehensible to the human eye and is inaccessible to the human mind. The encounter is possible because through divine grace and personal discipline, prayer and purification, the committed Christian acquires 'spiritual senses' in and by which God becomes accessible to him. Communion with God is then a constant ascent 'from glory to glory', with each step in the ascent an ascent into a richer, deeper encounter with the inexhaustibility of God, who is pure and true Love.

After recounting the virtuous life of Moses, Gregory moves on to contemplate that life. Here we find he interprets the Scripture in ways which have become uncommon in churches of the West today. He uses allegorical methods of interpretation in order to set forth spiritual and moral truths from the basic elements of the story. For example, the daughter of Pharaoh who adopted Moses is presented as pointing to profane philosophy to which a person can be strongly attached; in contrast, the light from the burning bush in the desert is interpreted as being the light of God's truth in the Gospel. It was the general view in the Church of his day that the primary aim of Scripture is to elevate the soul to God.

The actual style and content of this book is so different to the typical Western book on the spiritual life that a reader unfamiliar with Greek patristic theology/teaching could easily be deterred. This would be regrettable as the Eastern Christian approach can often be the very door through which the zealous soul can enter to find the living God.

However, not everything that Gregory writes is mysterious. This is how the book ends:

> This is true perfection: not to avoid a wicked life because like slaves we fear punishment, nor to do good works because we hope for rewards, as if cashing in on the virtuous life by some business-like and contractual arrangement. On the contrary, disregarding all those things for which we hope and which have been reserved by promise, we regard falling from God's friendship as the only thing dreadful and we consider becoming God's friend the only thing worthy of honour and desire.

41

The Triads

GREGORY PALAMAS
(1296–1359)

A monk, archbishop and theologian, Gregory Palamas became the great defender of the form of spirituality known as *hesychia* – the life of hermits dedicated to contemplation and prayer. His defence which appeared in three groups of three books (thus *The Triads*) between 1338 and 1341 is entitled *For the Defence of Those who practice Sacred Quietude (i.e. Hesychia)*. He was wholly supported by the monks of Mount Athos in his writings which were made necessary by the criticism of Barlaam of Calabria.

Many Christians only know *hesychia* as involving the reciting of the Jesus Prayer ('Lord Jesus Christ, have mercy on me a sinner') with the mind-in-the-heart. However, it is a way of experiencing God in meditative and contemplative prayer, which involves the whole person, body and soul; and it is much easier to appreciate if one has stayed at a Greek monastery!

Gregory Palamas insisted that we experience God in true prayer in soul and body – not soul alone. He explained that in the Incarnation the Word of God deified humanity:

So similarly in spiritual man, the grace of the Spirit, transmitted to the body, through the soul, grants to the body also the experiences of things divine, and allows it the same blessed experiences as the soul undergoes.

The deification of the body is seen for example in the way that the face of Stephen, the first martyr, shone when he saw the exalted Lord Jesus in a vision. Thus, because of the unity of body and soul and the experience of God by the whole person, the physical exercises (e.g. breathing to the rhythm of the prayer) used by the monks are justified.

He explained and defended the claim of the monks to 'see' the Divine Light in contemplative prayer:

> Do you not see how this light shines even now in the hearts of the faithful and perfect? Do you not see how it is superior to the light of knowledge? It has nothing to do with that which comes from studying Greek philosophy . . . This light of contemplation even differs from the light that comes from the Holy Scriptures. whose light may be compared to 'a lamp that shines in an obscure place', whereas the light of mystical contemplation is compared to the star of the morning which shines in full daylight, that it to say, to the sun.

It is the Light which shone in and through Christ when he was transfigured on the mountain.

Certainly this is a book for those who either having begun to use the Jesus Prayer seriously or want to discover its fuller spirituality or who are attracted by hesychasm and want to know more. See also *Philokalia* of St Macarius and St Nicodemus (p. 129).

42

Manual for Interior Souls

JOHN NICHOLAS GROU S.J.
(1731–1803)

This collection of sixty-three short papers was written by Père Grou just before he fled from Paris to England for safety during the French Revolution. They contain the substance of the spiritual direction and guidance he had been giving to those who came secretly to him in those troubled days, as well as material he wrote originally for the Archbishop of Paris.

The range of the subjects is comprehensive: the theological knowledge and spiritual insight are deep, but the collection is not difficult to read. There are careful definitions of devotion and virtue as well as guidance as to how to be truly devoted to God and to cultivate the virtues. There are explanations of how temptations arise and how they are to be faced as well as teaching on how to trust in God, rest in him, fear and love him, and abandon oneself entirely to him, and much more beside!

In this extract he teaches what Christians need to, but may not want, to hear:

> We must not forget that one of the greatest secrets of the spiritual life is that the Holy Spirit leads us in it not only by light and sweetness, by consolations, tendernesses, and facility of prayer, but also by obscurities and blindness, by insensibility, troubles, anguish of soul, sorrow and desolation, and often the rebellion of all our evil passions

and tempers . . . This crucified state is necessary for us, is good, is best and safest and will bring us more sooner to the height of perfection (maturity). A soul that is really enlightened thinks very highly of this conduct of God when he permits her to be tried by creatures and overwhelmed with temptations and desolations; and she understands quite well that these are favours rather than hardships and she would rather die upon the cross of Calvary than live in the sweetness of Tabor.

Here he speaks of what is often called purgation of the soul. But he has much also to say – which is uplifting to read and consider – on the illumination of the soul and of its yearning after communion with God, the Fountain of Love.

This is a book to which a person who is maturing in Christ can often turn for help and encouragement for its insights can function as a kind of pastoral counsellor or spiritual director. In fact it has a piece on what to look for and expect in a spiritual director! However, be warned, he admits that true directors of souls are rare and not easily found. Yet it is necessary he writes, 'to have a director because the greatest mistake of all is to wish to guide ourselves, and the greatest delusion we can fall into is to think we are in a fit state to guide ourselves.' Read also his *Meditations on the Love of God*, *Marks of True Devotion*, and *Spiritual Maxims*.

43

The Christian in Complete Armour

WILLIAM GURNALL
(1616–1679)

Gurnall was Rector of Lavenham, a pretty Suffolk village, for thirty-five years. He was one of those clergymen of Puritan persuasion who actually conformed to the Act of Uniformity of 1662, thereby retaining his rectory under Charles II.

We remember him for one book, an exceedingly fine – if rather long – book which is an explanation of St Paul's teaching in Ephesians 6:10–20 about the armour supplied by God to the Christian who is fighting Christ's battle against Satanic forces in the world. *The Christian in Complete Armour* was written after long years of study, reflection and the care of souls and certainly takes most seriously the presence and power of Satan in God's world, in the Church, and in human lives.

He deals with such topics as the wiles and power of Satan; how Satan corrupts the believer by error and pride; how to defeat the stratagems of Satan; the power and importance of genuine faith in God through the Lord Jesus and the power of faith over temptations; the use of the sacred Scriptures, the Word of God; the place and power of prayer in the battle with Satan; and what it is to pray in the Spirit and to make intercessions for others.

While he presents a dramatic and powerful portrait of the Christian life as warfare against spiritual forces, he does not neglect other models of the Christian life. For example, the

Christian is a pilgrim on route to Mount Zion:

> The sincere Christian is progressive – never at his journey's end till he gets to heaven. This keeps him always in motion, advancing in his desires and endeavours forward: he is thankful for little graces but not content with great measures of grace . . . Thus the sincere soul thinks it not enough to receive a little, now and then, of grace and comfort, from heaven by trading and holding commerce at a distance with God in his ordinances here below; but projects and meditates a conquest of that holy land, and blessed place, from whence such rich commodities come, that he may drink the wine of that kingdom in that kingdom. This raiseth the soul to high and noble enterprises – how it may attain to further degrees of graces every day more and more than another, and so climb nearer and nearer to heaven.

This recalls for us the great emphasis in the spirituality of the seventeenth century on meditating upon Christ in heaven in order rightly to be able to live for Christ in the world, and do battle with evil and sin in this world.

The interest in Gurnall's book has been so great recently that one publisher is now offering it in a modernised abridgement. However, the reprinted original may still be the best to read.

44

A Short Method of Prayer

MADAME GUYON
(1648–1717)

Unhappy in her marriage to Jacques Guyon, Jeannne-Marie (née Bouvier de la Motte) looked for comfort in the serious practice of Christianity. Made to love much, and finding nothing to love around her, she gave her love to God, first as a married woman and then, after her husband's death in 1676, as a widow.

Speaking of her conversion in 1668 she wrote: 'O my Lord, you were within my heart, and you asked of me only that I should return within, in order that I might feel your presence. O infinite Goodness, you were so near, and I, running here and there to seek you, found you not!'

In 1685 she published her *Moyen court et très facile pour l'oraison* (known in English as *A short and very easy method of prayer*). In this she attempted to make available to everyone an easy way of prayer that would lead to the pure contemplation of God.

Some persons when they hear of the prayer of quiet falsely imagine that the soul remains stupid, dead and inactive. But unquestionably it acts therein, more nobly and more extensively than it had ever done before, for God himself is the mover and the soul now acts by the agency of his Spirit . . . Instead, then, of prompting idleness, we promote the highest activity, by inculcating a total dependence on the

Spirit of God as our moving principle, for in him we live and move and have our being . . . Our activity should, therefore, consist in endeavouring to acquire and maintain such a state as may be most susceptible of divine impressions, most flexile to all the operations of the Eternal Word. Whilst a tablet is unsteady, the painter is unable to delineate a true copy; so every act of our own selfish and proper spirit is productive of false and erroneous lineaments, it interrupts the work and defeats the design of this Adorable Artist.

This book – and others – were much appreciated amongst English-speaking evangelicals (for example John Wesley) primarily, it seems, because of the teaching on total self-abandonment to the will of God, with which this form of prayer is intimately linked.

In France she became the friend and teacher of Archbishop Fénelon (whose *Letters* are fine spiritual reading). He defended her when she was accused of false teaching in promoting Quietism, the mysticism which requires complete passivity to God's will. In fact, she went to prison several times accused of heresy. What she teaches (and may be read in her *Works* in thirty-nine volumes) is difficult to understand and often not in guarded language. However, her book on prayer which has proved so popular and influential does not suffer too much from vagueness of language. When used by people in a sound Catholic or Protestant tradition it teaches how to experience God in prayer and how to pass on from saying prayers to enjoying living communion with God.

45

The Temple

GEORGE HERBERT
(1593–1633)

After a short and brilliant academic career at Cambridge, Herbert married, was ordained and became the rector of Bremerton. He gave himself unreservedly to the calling of a pastor and his high ideals may be read, with much profit, in his *A Priest to the Temple, or a Country Parson*. Virtually all his poetry (written between 1629 and 1663) except his Latin verses is to be found in *The Temple*, and his reputation as a poet rests upon this remarkable collection, published posthumously in 1633. His scrupulous craftsmanship brought clarity to the expression of arresting thoughts and unusual images, often in very short poems; also (and this is much less noticed today) the poems commend a classical, ordered, Anglican piety which is firmly rooted in the Scriptures and the reformed Catholic tradition.

The architectural setting of the temple (parish church) is used as a framework in which to set the one hundred and sixty-two poems. These relate to the individual before God as well as the place of the individual in the universal Church. Perhaps the most famous one is that which ends the collection and is entitled 'Love', of which the first stanza is:

> Love bade me welcome: yet my soul drew back,
>   Guiltie of dust and sinne.
> But quick-ey's Love, observing me grow slack

From my first entrance in,
Drew nearer to me, sweetly questioning,
If I lacked anything.

There are others which have been used as hymns – 'King of Glory, King of Peace, I will love thee', and 'Teach me my God and King, in all things thee to see'. It is a remarkable collection which will appeal especially to those who are moved more by poetry than prose in their search for an authentically Christian spirituality.

In his preface to *The Temple*, Nicholas Ferrar of the Little Gidding Community told the readers that Herbert would in ordinary speech always add, after making mention of the name of Jesus Christ, 'my Master'. Then he explained that 'next to God, he loved that which God himself has magnified above all things, that is, his Word; so as he has been heard to make solemn protestation that he would not part with one leaf thereof for the whole world, if it were offered to him in exchange.' As to his loyalty as an Anglican he wrote that his 'obedience and conformity to the Church and the discipline thereof was singularly remarkable. Though he abounded in private devotions, yet he went every morning and evening with his family to the church; and by his example, exhortations and encouragements drew the greater part of his parishioners to accompany him daily in the public celebration of Divine Service.'

Herbert's own motto was: 'Less than the least of God's mercies.'

46

The Ladder of Perfection

WALTER HILTON
(d. 1396)

This was one of the first books to be printed in England – in 1494; and both before and since that date it has enjoyed a wide and enduring influence as a devotional classic. All we know about Hilton, apart from what he has written in his books is that he was a Canon Regular of Saint Augustine at the priory of St Peter at Thurgarton, near Southwell.

The work is in fact two books written separately but put together later. In them there is a gradual unfolding of the progress of the soul through the way of purgation to illumination by God and contemplative union with him in love. This is presented with teaching on the nature and practice of prayer. The spirituality is in the tradition of Augustine of Hippo and Bernard of Clairvaux and finds its centre in Jesus.

Hilton made it clear that:

> The purpose of prayer is not to inform our Lord what you desire for he knows all your needs. It is to render you able and ready to receive the grace which our Lord will freely give you. The grace cannot be experienced until you have been refined and purified by the fire of desire in devout prayer. For although prayer is not the cause for which our Lord gives grace, it is nevertheless the means by which grace, freely given, comes to the soul.

When praying it is important, he explained, to detach your

heart and withdraw your mind from all earthly things:

> If, when you pray, your heart is lightened, helped, and freed
> from the burden of all worldly thoughts and affections, and
> rises up in the power of the Spirit to a spiritual delight in
> his presence so that you are scarcely conscious of earthly
> things or are little distracted by them, then you are praying
> well. For prayer is nothing other than the ascent of the heart
> to God, and its withdrawal from all earthly thoughts.
> Therefore prayer is compared to fire, which of its own nature
> always leaves the earth and leaps into the air. Similarly,
> prayerful desire, when touched and kindled by the spiritual
> fire of God, constantly leaps upwards to him from whom
> it comes.

Then he proceeds to describe the 'fire of love' which the devout
experience in prayer. The fire is felt in their souls and causes
the body to feel warm: however, it is caused by the spiritual
desire of the soul and is not in its origin a physical reality at
all. Much later in the treatise, in the second book, he has a
chapter entitled, 'How Jesus is heaven to the soul, and why
he is called Fire.'

So the maturing soul climbs the ladder of ascent to
perfection: and, as Hilton also explains, the pilgrim travels
forwards glimpsing Jerusalem and moving through darkness
and difficulty to Jesus, the Lamb in the City.

47

Letters to a Niece

BARON FRIEDRICH VON HÜGEL
(1852–1925)

A Roman Catholic born in Austria of an Austrian father and
Scottish mother, von Hügel lived in England from the age of
fifteen. However, he had European interests and wrote various
books on the philosophy of religion as well as a major study
of Catherine of Genoa. He was also a guide and encourager
of souls both in person and through correspondence. In fact
he was one of the dying race of thoughtful correspondents!
On his tombstone is the simple inscription: 'Whom have I in
heaven but Thee?'

His niece was Gwendolen Greene who edited the *Letters* for
publication and wrote an important introduction. She said this
of the Baron:

> I cannot attempt to describe my uncle. Many can do that so
> much better than I. I am dominated and absorbed by his
> greatness. He seems to me as rich and large as the world.
> I am lost in his depth, silenced by his nobility. I remember
> his words to me about great things: 'Be silent about great
> things; let them grow inside you. Never discuss them:
> discussion is so limiting and distracting. It makes things grow
> smaller. You think you swallow things when they ought to
> swallow you. Before all greatness, be silent – in art, music,
> in religion: silence.' And so before him I must be silent, and
> let him speak for himself.

So she presents his letters written between 1918 and 1924, for others to read.

Of course, some of them make greater sense if the reader knows a little of the history and culture of the period, for the spiritual guidance is offered within general guidance on life and comments on current events. Here is a paragraph on worldliness:

As to worldliness – well, yes my Gwen, it is a thoroughly vulgar thing, especially when we remember the regal call of our souls. There is, however, one consolation about this – worldliness is a less dangerous foe of the spiritual life than is brooding and self-occupation of the wrong, weakening sort. Nothing ousts the sense of God's presence so thoroughly as the soul's dialogues with itself – when these are grumblings, grievances, etc. But, of course, the ideal is to do without worldliness or brooding. I say all this, whilst confident that you do not class a right amount of (and kind of) sociability and of pleasure in it, as worldliness. Of course, such social activity and pleasure is right, and indeed a duty and a help to God.

The Baron's spirituality was such that he was able to enjoy nature, art and music and social encounters. He was a mystic who went about, as it has been said, with his eyes open! Read also his *Selected Letters* (1927).

48

Noah's Ark

HUGH OF ST VICTOR
(1096–1141)

The Abbey of St Victor, home of the Augustinian Canons Regular in Paris, flourished under Hugh. There was spiritual and intellectual fervour and contemplative prayer was united with intensive intellectual pursuits. Hugh directed studies here from 1133 and achieved an international reputation for his teaching and writing.

This book is built around three medieval methods of interpreting Scripture – the literal, the allegorical and the drawing of moral meanings from the writings. But it begins with a discussion occasioned by reflection on the famous statement of St Augustine that the human heart is always restless until it finds its true rest in God. Here is how Hugh sets out the problem which God in grace will solve through Christ and by the Holy Spirit:

The first man was so created that if he had not sinned he would always have beheld in present contemplation his Creator's face, and by always seeing him would have loved him always, and by loving him would have clung close to him, and by clinging close to him who was eternal would have possessed life without end. Evidently the one true good of man was perfect knowledge of his creator.

But this state of affairs did not last long and for his sin 'man

103

was struck with the blindness of ignorance and passed from that intimate light of contemplation; and he inclined his mind to earthly desires, and he began to forget the sweetness of the divine.' He became a wanderer and a fugitive: 'a wanderer because of disordered concupiscence; and a fugitive, through guilty conscience.' Thus the heart of man, once kept secure in the divine love and by loving the true One, now began to be swayed here and there through earthly and worldly desires.

Such is the problem. Noah's Ark is the symbol of the saving work of God whereby he restores to human beings that knowledge of himself which is first necessary if they are to be able ever to love him again. The path into this knowledge is through meditation upon Scripture. 'If we have begun to live persistently in our own heart through the practice of meditation, we have already in a manner ceased to belong to time; and, having become dead as it were to the world, we are living inwardly with God.' Yet such meditation and contemplation developing from it must lead to humility and to the union in love with God. In his own meditations of the 'tree of wisdom', which make up a large part of this book, Hugh offers penetrating analyses of and comments on human thinking and its relationship to true virtue and charity. He concludes that each true Christian ought to live in the ark which God creates in his soul in order that he might not love the world and desire what it offers, but rather desire, know and love God and, in his love, serve the world.

49

Epistles

IGNATIUS OF ANTIOCH
(c.35–c.107)

Ignatius was chief pastor and bishop of the church in Antioch. At that time in Roman history the provinces of the Empire were required to provide criminals for the circus in Rome where they were thrown to the wild beasts for the amusement of the crowd. Ignatius had broken Roman law by his total faithfulness to the confession of Christ and was taken to Rome under guard to suffer this fate. However, on the long journey, he was able to meet with Christians and write letters to the churches in six places (Ephesus, Magnesia, Tralles, Rome, Philaelphia and Smyrna) as well as a personal letter to Polycarp (see p. 131). He knew he was going to Rome to be a martyr for Jesus and this thought was prominent in his mind as he journeyed.

Ignatius has been given great eminence in the Church and his *Epistles* have been read and treasured for three reasons. First, the man himself is revealed by the letters to be wise, fearless, holy, prayerful and evangelistic. Secondly, his theology has much to say about the importance of the pastor as spiritual guide, the unity of the Christian community and the glory of martyrdom. Thirdly, the way he speaks of martyrdom (and the accounts of his own death) has inspired thousands to be ready (even to desire) to be martyrs for Jesus.

Here is how he addressed his fellow Christians in Rome, where he was going as a prisoner. He tells them that he is truly in earnest about dying for Christ and asks them not to do anything to try to prevent his becoming a martyr:

Pray leave me to be a meal for the beasts, for it is they who can provide my way to God. I am his wheat, ground fine by lions' teeth to be made pure bread for Christ. Better still, incite the creatures to become a sepulchre for me; let them not leave the smallest scrap of my flesh, so that I need not be a burden to anyone after I fall asleep. When there is no trace of my body left for the world to see, then I shall truly be Jesus Christ's disciple. So intercede with Christ for me, that through the wild beasts I may be made a sacrifice to God. I am not issuing orders to you, as though I were a Peter or Paul. They were apostles and I am a condemned criminal . . . For the present these chains are schooling me to have done with earthly desires.

He continued his plea in a similar vein but ended the letter asking their prayers for the church he had left behind. 'Remember the church of Syria in your prayers: it has God for its pastor now, in place of myself, and Jesus Christ alone will have oversight of it – he, and your own love.'

These *Epistles* are very important for they give us an insight into the dynamic of Christianity only forty or so years after the death of most of the apostles.

50

The Spiritual Exercises

IGNATIUS OF LOYOLA
(c.1492–1556)

Ignatius became the first Superior-General of the Society of Jesus (Jesuits). He was intending a career in the military and at court but after being injured in war he experienced a thorough conversion. During his convalescence at Manresa in 1523 he began to write the *Spiritual Exercises* but the text was not finally ready until 1548, eight years after the Jesuit Order had been founded.

The book is divided into four parts, each part containing material which is intended to be used during one week. In the first week there is the examination of conscience and set meditations on our sins, hell and the kingdom of Christ. During the second week there is contemplation (imaginative meditation) on the Christ of the Gospels and directions as to making a right choice in life. For both the third and fourth week there are more contemplations ending with instruction on several methods of prayer. To all the material are added various rules – for discernment of spirits, distribution of alms, and for thinking with the Church.

Ignatius explained in his first paragraph that the term 'spiritual exercises' meant 'every method of examination of conscience, of meditation, of contemplation, of vocal and mental prayer, and of other spiritual activities'. They represent 'every way of preparing and disposing the soul to rid itself of all inordinate attachments, and, after their removal, of seeking and finding the will of God in the disposition of our life for the salvation of our soul'. He intended the book for those who were directing retreats and especially for Jesuit priests who were directing individual retreats for those who were thinking of becoming Jesuits. Although for many years the book has been available to the general public in a variety of translations, it was certainly not planned for a general readership. In fact in their original form the *Exercises* reflect the militant spirituality of the Roman Catholic Counter-Reformation with emphasis upon obedience and the specific guidance of a spiritual director.

However, the *Exercises* were never intended to be used rigidly. Ignatius insisted that they must be adapted to the condition of the one who is to engage in them, that is, to his age, education and talent. Thus exercises he could not easily bear, or from which he would derive no profit, should not be given to 'one with little natural ability or of little physical strength.' They were intended to be used as part of the way God made clear the vocation of retreatant.

Today, an Ignatian retreat can refer either to a full retreat or it may refer to a short retreat where the emphasis is upon using all the senses in contemplating Jesus at various points in his life, passion, crucifixion and resurrection with suitable application to life and appropriate self-examination.

(To avoid confusion it is useful to know that Ignatius uses the word contemplation of pictorial imaginative meditation – not of a higher form of prayer than meditation.)

51

Lives of Early Methodist Preachers

EDITED BY THOMAS JACKSON
(1783–1873)

The first generation of Methodist preachers were a remarkable group of men who were wholly devoted to their task and whose lives vibrate with joy and holiness. It is stimulating to read their stories, as told by themselves, for in them are the central themes of Methodist spirituality, visibly portrayed.

In 1778 John Wesley founded the *Arminian Magazine* (not the best choice of title!) He asked some of his preachers to submit vignettes of their pilgrimage of grace. These were highly prized at the time and in 1837 Thomas Jackson, a president of the Wesleyan Conference, began to publish some of these autobiographical accounts under the title of *The Lives of Early Methodist Preachers*. The first edition was in three volumes (1837–38) and the fourth (with excellent index) was in six volumes (1871). Then, with a changed title and with some extra material and annotations, John Telford brought out a new edition in seven small volumes under the title, *Wesley's Veterans: Lives of Early Methodist Preachers told by themselves* (1912–1914). This contained thirty-six lives.

Thomas Rankin was a Scot who was converted through the preaching of George Whitefield and later served as Wesley's superintendent in America (1773–78). Here is how he described his quest for Christian perfection (see *Plain Account of Christian Perfection*, by John Wesley, p.193), which began in the fellowship of the class meeting, a characteristic feature of

Methodist discipline and spirituality:

As soon as the meeting was finished, I went home, and retired to private prayer; but all was darkness and painful distress. I found no intercourse with heaven, and faith and prayer seemed to have lost their wings. For five days and five nights I went through such distress of soul as made sleep, the desire for food, depart from me. I could attend to nothing but my painful feelings, and mourn and weep. On the fifth day two friends called to see me, and we joined in prayer, and I found more liberty than I had experienced during the time of this painful distress. As soon as my friends were gone, I fell down on my knees, and continued in prayer till I went to bed. I now found a degree of sweetness and communion with my Lord once more; and I closed my eyes with the pleasing sensation. I awoke very early next morning, and with a change in my feelings, that I could scarce allow myself time to dress before I fell on my knees to praise God; and when on my knees, I had such a view of the goodness and love of God as almost overcame every power of body and soul.

This time of crisis with a sense of being filled by or immersed in the love and joy of the Lord is central to the experience of the 'second blessing'. Its immediate result is to send a person forth in the name of Jesus to declare the Gospel in word and deed.

110

52

Prayers for Families

BENJAMIN JENKS
(1646–1724)

AND CHARLES SIMEON
(1759–1836)

Jenks was Rector of Harley in Shropshire where he produced several books on meditation and prayer which were highly appreciated. *Prayers and Offices of Devotion for Families* was discovered by Evangelicals in the Church of England in the early nineteenth century and brought back into print. Charles Simeon of Cambridge, perhaps the most influential of Anglican evangelical clergymen in the first half of the nineteenth century, was greatly impressed by the book and prepared an edition of it himself, suitable for his own times.

In his preface Simeon explained that he had 'for many years considered the book as an exceedingly rich treasure to the Church of God. Its distinguishing excellency is that by far the greater part of the prayers appear to have been prayed and not merely written.' He went on to claim that 'there is a spirit of humiliation in them which is admirably suited to express the sentiments of a contrite heart. There is also a fervour of devotion in them, which can scarcely fail of kindling a corresponding flame in the breasts of those who use them.'

Of course what the book first witnesses to is the importance placed on family prayer within the home by pastors. Comprehensive prayers are provided for use each morning and each evening of the week. These can be the model for prayers or can be used as written. Their origin is in the home of Jenks with his own family, and in the homes of parishioners. Then there are prayers for the Lord's Day, before and after receiving Holy Communion, festival times like Christmas and Easter, times of sickness, prosperity and adversity, increasing maturity and sanctification in Christ, members of society and leaders of government, the Church of God, people in need, times of thanksgiving for temporal and spiritual blessings.

Its great value is that it can be used as a book of prayers to be prayed, as a book of prayers to use as meditations in preparation for one's own prayers, or as guidelines to help the framing of one's own extempore or written public prayers as well as private devotions. All the prayers are too long for any single one to be quoted here in full. It may be said that while they have an evangelical flavour (which gives them warmth) they are also much influenced by the immersion of the author and editor in the language and spirit of the Book of Common Prayer, which Simeon described as 'that excellent Liturgy'.

I have prepared a paperback edition for modern families with the title, *Family Prayers* (Hodder) because the valuable older editions are difficult to find. The contents of the book can do much to help the development of appropriate thoughts and language in prayer used in the home, the fellowship group and in the prayers used in congregational worship.

53

The Ascent of Mount Carmel and The Dark Night

JOHN OF THE CROSS
(1542–1591)

These two treatises by the Spanish Carmelite poet, saint and mystic, are best taken together because they are a commentary on his poem, *Dark Night*, whose opening stanzas are:

> On a dark secret night,
> starving for love and deep in flame,
>   O happy lucky flight!
>   unseen I slipped away,
> my house at last was calm and safe.

> Blackly free from light
> disguised and down a secret way,
>   O happy lucky flight!
>   in darkness I escaped,
> my house at last was calm and safe.

> On that happy night-in
> secret; no one saw me through the dark –
>   and I saw nothing then,
>   no other light to mark
> the way but fire pounding my heart.

The Ascent of Mount Carmel is a prose commentary on the first

113

two stanzas, dealing with the active night of the senses and the active night of the spirit. *The Dark Night* is also a prose commentary on stanzas one, two and three, and it deals with the passive nights of sense and spirit.

The word 'night' is used with different meanings as the theme develops. First it means suffering, the pain caused by the putting to death of our sense desires and sensual appetites. Secondly, it means the journey of faith, with its darkness to the natural understanding. In the third place, night is the dispossession of the memory, which is purified of distinct forms, images or ideas which are not of God, by the practice of the virtue of hope. Finally, in the Ascent it is the purification of the will of all unruly affections, feelings or emotions, by the virtue of charity. Then in the Dark Night we discover that the night is God's loving communication to the soul; because it is accompanied by passive purification of the spirit; it is intensely painful to the soul − hence a 'night'.

Obviously, these two books are not for beginners but for those who want to mature in their relationship with the Lord Jesus and who want to be led into a deeper prayer-life. They are perhaps best read after reading Teresa of Avila, who was a close friend of John of the Cross.

John was canonized in 1726 and declared a Doctor of the Church in 1926. This century has witnessed a growing appreciation of his poetry and his treatises have become influential in spiritual formation for Christians in various traditions.

54

Revelations of Divine Love

JULIAN OF NORWICH
(c.1342–c.1413)

Little is known of Julian's life except that she probably lived as an anchoress outside the walls of St Julian's Church, Norwich. However, she is the most widely read and influential mystic of the English spiritual tradition and is by her book the encourager and consoler of thousands. At the age of thirty according to her own account, on 8th May, 1373, she received a series of fifteen revelations while in a state of ecstasy. A further vision followed the next day. She meditated upon these for the next twenty or so years before writing her book, *The Sixteen Revelations of Divine Love*, in homely, lively, practical and imaginative language. Despite her disclaimer, 'I am a woman, unlettered, feeble and frail' her book is in vigorous English prose. The main theme of the book is the understanding of sin and sorrow in the world in the light of the love of God. Her answer is in the much quoted words: 'All will be well, all manner of things will be well.'

With the arrival of the feminist movement and the call by some people to use feminine images of God, Julian's writing has become of even greater interest to the modern generation. This is because she uses motherhood as a way of describing God's gracious relationship to human beings. Her use of this image comes not in the visions themselves but in her comments or meditations on the first fourteen of them (chapters 58 – 62). In fact it is the eternal Son of God (in and by whom human beings were created and through whom they are redeemed) whom she particularly calls 'our Mother'. She wrote in chapter 58:

> I saw that the Second person (of the Trinity) who is our Mother with regard to our essential being, has become our Mother in regard to our physical nature too, for God has made us in two parts: essential being, and physical nature. Our essential being is our higher nature which is in the keeping of our Father, God almighty. When our essential being was made the Second Person of the Trinity was our natural mother, and in him we are rooted and grounded. But he is also our Mother out of mercy because he took our physical nature. So our Mother in whom our two natures are undivided is a mother to us in different ways. In our Mother, Christ, we prosper and develop; in his mercy he corrects and restores us; and by the power of his passion, death and resurrection he unites us to our essential being. That is how our Mother works in mercy for all his children who are yielding and obedient to him.

This is intriguing and there are some women who claim that using an image like this helps them to worship God sincerely.

There is much in Julian apart from this theme; for example, her lively images from nature – especially that of the hazelnut (ch. 5) – give an ecological slant to her spirituality. She makes for stimulating reading, meditation and prayer.

55

Purity of Heart is to Will One Thing

SØREN AABY KIERKEGAARD
(1813–1855)

Born in Copenhagen into a wealthy family, the seventh son of a wool-merchant, Kierkegaard remained in the city for virtually all his life. From childhood he was separated from others both by genius and by suffering. His father's presentation of Lutheran religion instilled in him a dread of God and at university he had a moral and mental crisis which he described as 'the great earthquake'. He decided not to marry the girl whom he loved and not to be ordained into the State Church. Then he accepted the burden of isolation and dedicated his life to the task of correcting certain spiritual misdirections in the Christian religion of his day. Much of what he wrote attempted to make people aware that they were human creatures made by God in order to have a right and fruitful relationship with him. He asked them to reflect upon and consider their actual existence (he is often called the father of existentialism) as being given to them by God so that they would offer it back to him in the name of Jesus Christ, the Saviour.

Though it was never preached, *Purity of Heart* is in the form of a long, written sermon with a text, divisions and application. It was designed as a preparation for the office of confession but this fact does not limit its usefulness, for confession can arise in the heart at any time. The scriptural text from which he began is James 4:8, 'Come near to God and he will come

117

near to you. Wash your hands you sinners, and purify your hearts you double-minded.'

In the preface Kierkegaard tells us for whom the book is written: It is in search of that solitary 'individual' to whom it wholly abandons itself, by whom it wishes to be received as if it had arisen within his own heart'. Then in the first part of the sermon we learn that to will one thing, which is to will the Good, which is to will the will of God, is what life ought to be all about.

'Father in heaven! What is a man without thee! What is all that he knows, vast accumulation though it be, but a chipped fragment if he does not know thee! What is all his striving, could it even encompass the whole world, but a half-finished work if it does not know Thee: Thee the One, who art one thing and who art all! So may thou give to the intellect, wisdom to comprehend that one thing; to the heart, sincerity to receive this understanding; to the will, purity that wills to will one thing. In prosperity may thou grant perseverance to will one thing; amid distractions, collectedness to will one thing; in suffering, patience to will one thing . . .'

To will one thing is as necessary for the old as for the young but all too often this willing is absent.

The sermon makes clear how purity of heart, willing the will of God alone may be achieved. A demanding but rewarding book, especially for those who like their minds to be stretched in the seeking of the Lord God.

56

A Serious Call to a Devout and Holy Life

WILLIAM LAW
(1686–1761)

Law refused to take the oath of loyalty to George I in 1714. He was deprived of his Fellowship at Emmanuel College, Cambridge, and spent the rest of his life first at Putney with the Gibbon family and then at King's Cliffe in Northamptonshire where he had been born. Without either teaching or ecclesiastical duties in the Church, he gave himself both to writing and to practical service of poor people. Some of his books remain in print and he is highly regarded as a writer on the spiritual life.

A Serious Call (1728) is truly serious – it is not for the weak or faint-hearted but for those who take the call to be holy as the most important of all calls. Though Anglican in spirit and character it owes much to the Catholic tradition with its use of the canonical hours, the commendation of the benefits of the cloistered life, and special reverence for the Blessed Virgin Mary. He works on the assumption that the shallow formalism of much of the religion of his day must be rejected and replaced by such serious propositions as that life on earth is truly a preparation for eternity, that every Christian is a potential saint, and that the whole life of a Christian must be entirely dedicated to God for Christ's sake. All frivolity and triviality must be abandoned and dedication and discipline and devotion must be the way of life. There is guidance on self-examination, prayer, meditation and how to prepare for meeting the Lord

God at death. And there are penetrating comparisons between pseudo and genuine Christian discipleship.

Law does not write in a vivid or colourful way but in a plain and logical manner. What he says is clear and, to those with searching minds, easy to grasp and understand. This is why it has influenced so many people including such Evangelical leaders as John Wesley and George Whitefield. Of course it is not a perfect book: it lacks the spirit of joyful celebration and has too little to say of the gracious work of God which enables the true disciple to live the ascetic, disciplined, godly and devout life in the spirit of Christian charity. However, for what it sets out to do, it is a classic and still has the power to move any Christian reader to a greater devotion to the Lord Jesus. To Law it was clear that 'Christianity is a calling that puts an end to all other callings' and that 'Devotion signifies a life given, or devoted, entirely to God'.

His *Christian Perfection* (1726) has much of the same character as *A Serious Call*. However, his later works, *The Spirit of Prayer* (1749) and *The Spirit of Love* (1752) are very different and have a mystical quality which owes much to the writings of Jacob Boehme (an unorthodox German Lutheran mystic), and which have been much appreciated by Quakers. It is, however, *A Serious Call* which has stood the test of the years and still draws many readers to it.

57

The Practice of the Presence of God

BROTHER LAWRENCE OF THE RESURRECTION
(1611–1691)

Nicholas Herman was born in Lorraine and became a soldier when only a teenager. He was wounded and left the army with a permanent disability. Later in life he was received in the Order of Discalced (Barefoot) Carmelites, named from Elijah's retreat on Mount Carmel, at the Parisian monastery. As Frère Laurent he lived an uneventful life for thirty years as a cook to the friars. He wrote nothing apart from a few notes and letters and he would not have been known at all outside his Order were it not for the Abbé Joseph de Beaufort.

The Abbé, vicar-general of Cardinal de Noailles, collected Lawrence's literary remains, which were few, and added to them his own accounts of the conversations he had with him between August 1666 and November 1667. He published this material in two volumes entitled *Maximes spirituelles* (1692) and *Moeurs et entretiens du F. Laurent* (1694). This century, these have been published as one volume with the title *La Pratique de la presence de Dieu* and in English translation as *The Practice of the Presence of God*.

Because he was a lay brother entirely dedicated to the Lord and wholly content to do what was required of him with commitment and joy, his practical spirituality is very attractive. It is very easy to understand even if it is difficult to imitate. The Abbé reports that:

Brother Lawrence often spoke to me with great fervour and frankness of his way of approaching God. He told me that it all amounted to one good act of renunciation of everything which we recognise does not lead to God, in order to habituate ourselves to an unbroken converse with him without mystery of artificiality. It is necessary only to realise that God is intimately present within us, to turn at every moment to him and ask for his help, recognise his will in all things doubtful, and to do well all that which we clearly see he requires of us, offering what we do to him before we do it, giving thanks for having done it afterwards. In this unbroken communion one is continually preoccupied with praising, worshipping and loving God for his infinite acts of loving-kindness and perfection.

Brother Lawrence explained in a letter to a lady that 'it is not needful always to be in church to be with God. We can make a chapel of our heart, to which we can withdraw from time to time to have a gentle, humble, loving communion with him. Everyone is able to have these familiar conversations with God, some more, some less – he knows our capabilities.' And to a priest he described in brief some of his experience of contemplative prayer. He would abide in God's holy presence by a simple attentiveness and an habitual, loving turning of his eyes on the Lord. This gave him great internal joy – more, he confessed, than that of a baby at its mother's breast.In fact such was the inexpressible happiness he felt in his condition that he was ready to call it 'the breasts of God'.

58

The Names of Christ

LUIS DE LÉON
(c.1527–1591)

Fray Luis, the Augustinian monk and professor of theology, is known for his commentaries on the Song of Songs and Job, for being chosen by the Carmelites as the editor of the writings of Teresa of Avila (see p. 171), for his mystical poems and for his masterpiece, *The Names of Christ* (as they are revealed in the Old Testament). Because of his advanced humanist, educational views he was even imprisoned for several years by the Spanish Inquisition. But his influence has lasted longer than the Inquisition and his *The Names* is now being read more than ever before. His wisdom, both down-to-earth and spiritual, makes him a man for all centuries.

The treatise is in three parts or books and its format is that of a dialogue between three characters (who may represent three aspects of his personality) concerning the revealed names of the Messiah in the Old Testament. Marcelo is the student of Scripture; Juliano is a scholastic critic and Sabino is a poet. Each name of Christ in the Old Testament (Branch, Face of God, the Way, the Shepherd, Mountain, Everlasting Father, Arm of God, King, Prince of Peace, Husband, Son of God, Lamb, Beloved, together with that of Jesus) is like a facet of a great diamond. The diamond itself cannot be appreciated and its worth known unless we lovingly study, contemplate, caress each facet in turn, after which we may attempt to comprehend the whole. In the same manner we should approach the Names of the Son of God.

In their discussion as to why Christ is given so many names Marcelo has this to say:

Christ is given so many names because of his limitless greatness and the treasury of his very rich perfections and with them the host of functions and other benefits which are born in him and spread over us. Just as they cannot be embraced by the soul's vision, so much less can a single word name them. Just as he who pours water in a bottle with a narrow and long neck does so drop by drop, so the Holy Spirit who knows the narrowness and poverty of our understanding does not give us that greatness all at once but offers it to us in drops, telling us, at times, something under one name, and some other thing at other times, under another name. Thus, there are innumerable names given to Christ in sacred Scriptures.

Of these only ten are studied in the treatise. The study of them enlightens the mind, warms the heart and moves the will towards true discipleship of this Christ, who is the Son of God in human form, the Word made flesh who has come to dwell among men. Sabino's poems at the ends of Books II and III sum up the response of devout souls to the exposition of the name of Jesus.

This is without doubt a fascinating book, providing insight into how a devout humanist came to Christ via the Bible.

59

The Freedom of a Christian

MARTIN LUTHER
(1483–1546)

Whatever Luther did, he did it with conviction and passion. In 1520, as the movement for the reform of the Church gathered momentum in Germany, Luther produced three treatises which together provide a dynamic statement of what is evangelical theology and spirituality and how it differs from the widespread and corrupt Catholicism of the time. It is a theology based primarily on the Bible but guided by the experience of the early Church.

In *An Open Letter to the German Nobility*, Luther called for the reform of the Church, attacked the authority of the Pope over secular rulers and set forth the priesthood of all believers in Christ. In *The Babylonian Captivity of the Church*, he attacked the sacramental system which had gained an excessive hold over people's lives and possessions, and he expounded an evangelical approach to the dominical sacraments. Finally, in *The Freedom of a Christian*, which was written in a decidedly conciliatory spirit, he explained the essence of Lutheran spirituality.

The Freedom of a Christian is built upon two statements:

A Christian is a perfectly free lord of all, subject to none.

A Christian is a perfectly dutiful servant of all, subject to all. Though these appear to contradict each other, in the Gospel they do fit together beautifully, claimed Luther.

Since a sinner has his sins forgiven and is placed in a right

125

relationship with God entirely through the love of Jesus, and since the believing sinner accepts this in faith recognising it wholly as a gift of grace, therefore the Christian is totally free from all need or compulsion to offer good works to God as the basis of his being forgiven: he is free from all dependence upon ecclesiastical or worldly mediation for his salvation. He looks to, and trusts in God in Christ alone, and is therefore subject to none except God himself.

However, the faith of the believing sinner which accepts the free gift of salvation in and through Jesus Christ is the very bond which unites the Christian to Christ through the invisible Holy Spirit. Now since Christ is the suffering servant who serves all people in love as their Saviour, those who are united to him in faith and love thereby share in his vocation to love all with the love of God. In this sense, being in Christ's Body, the Christian is a dutiful servant of all, subject to all.

This treatise proves, if proof is needed, that pure Lutheran teaching is wholly in favour of good works and sees them as absolutely necessary in the Christian life. Yet they are to be the fruit of faith since faith works in and through love. There is no such thing as being placed in a right relationship with God by faith, unless there is also the wholehearted commitment to love one's neighbour in the love of Christ. A truly heart-warming treatise!

60

A Simple Way to Pray

MARTIN LUTHER
(1483–1546)

In 1535 Luther, the dynamic German Protestant leader, was asked by his barber, Peter Beskendorf, for some guidance on how to prepare himself to pray and then to pray. So he went home and wrote a little treatise *A Simple Way to Pray, for a Good Friend*. What he says has been called a pure illustration of evangelical meditation.

Luther began with reference to his own experience: 'Whenever I feel that I have grown cold and disinclined to pray, because of other tasks and thoughts (for the flesh and the devil always prevent and hinder prayer) I take my little Psalter, hasten into my room, or, if it is during the day and I have time, to the church where others are gathered, and begin to say the Ten Commandments, the Creed, and then, if I have time, some words of Christ, Paul or the Psalms, saying them quietly to myself just as children do.'

When the heart has been warmed by this quiet reciting of parts of Scripture and the Creed, then Luther advises Beskendorf to kneel and pray to his heavenly Father asking his help and mercy in the name of Jesus Christ – Luther actually provides a prayer. Following this he suggests that his barber uses the Lord's Prayer phrase by phrase, thinking about and developing each one into an extended prayer; then the same (if there is time) with the Ten Commandments and the Creed. Examples of this meditatory prayer are supplied. To close his prayers Luther advises the giving of thanks, the confession of unbelief and unthankfulness, and petition for a right and steadfast faith in the Lord Jesus.

Perhaps it is best to read this little treatise at the same time as reading Luther's *Small Catechism* (1529), which is based upon the Ten Commandments, the Creed and the Lord's Prayer, for his aim is to integrate instruction and meditation, theology and prayer.

He was very much aware of the temptation to neglect prayer and to count activity as prayer and so he told his barber: 'We must be careful not to interpret prayer to mean all kinds of works which are necessary but not true prayer after all and thus in the end become careless, lazy, cold, and bored with prayer itself. For the devil who besets us is not lazy or careless, and our flesh is still all too active and eager to sin and inclined to be contrary to the spirit of prayer.' We must keep before us the call to 'pray without ceasing' and the need to fear God and keep his commandments as Psalm 1 makes clear, 'Blessed is the man who meditates on his Law day and night'.

Luther speaks to us from the heart and from personal experience. His way of meditating and praying is out of fashion today but perhaps the time has come for it to be revived, especially among those of evangelical persuasion!

61

Philokalia

COMPILED BY ST MACARIUS OF CORINTH
(1731–1805) AND
ST NICODEMUS OF THE HOLY MOUNTAIN
(1749–1809)

The *Philokalia* ('love for what is beautiful') is an anthology compiled by two leading members of a group who longed for spiritual renewal in Greek Orthodoxy in the eighteenth century. The writers are all from Orthodoxy and their dates range from the fourth to the fifteenth century. Apparently the original selection of texts was made by Macarius and then his work was revised by Nicodemus, who also added an introduction and notes on each writer. It was first published in Venice in 1782. Since then it has been translated into Romanian and other Slavonic languages including Russian. The English translation of the whole anthology has recently been completed and is available in five volumes. However, there are also extracts from the anthology in English translation published as one volume.

Among the writers within the *Phiokalia* are several who are listed separately in this book – for example Gregory Palamas and Maximus the Confessor. However, the anthology has texts from some thirty different writers and is the primary source-book for the tradition of spirituality in Orthodoxy known as hesychasm. This is a way of inner prayer and communion with God. It is associated with the use of the Jesus Prayer ('Lord Jesus Christ, Son of God, have mercy on me a sinner') especially when accompanied by a physical technique which involves the control of the breathing. It is prayer in which there is the experience of Divine Light, the very light which shone in and through Christ at his Transfiguration.

The collection covers a wide area – the elimination of evil thoughts, the cultivation of the virtues, the control and right ordering of the passions, the spiritual interpretation of the sacred Scriptures, meditating upon the natural world and on God's self-revelation, the true prayer of the heart, the Jesus Prayer and the control of breathing, the glory and grace of God in the face of Jesus Christ, deification of the whole person by the Incarnate Word through the Holy Spirit and other important themes. It contains the quintessence of the Orthodox monastic tradition, as it comes from Mount Athos and Mount Sinai.

Since the Second World War the *Philokalia* has become increasingly more widely read and more influential. It is not, however, easy reading for the average Western Christian. Before beginning it she or he ought perhaps to read an introduction to the Orthodox Church and tradition (e.g. by Kallistos Ware or John Meyendorff) as well as the little book *The Way of a Pilgrim* (for which see p. 207) which tells of one specific way that the Jesus Prayer' can be used. Perhaps the *Philokalia* is best seen as a source book to which the maturing Christian turns from time to time in order to read one or another of the thirty authors for specific guidance on particular points. To absorb its spirituality into Western Christianity takes time and patience!

62

The Martyrdom of Polycarp

MARCION
(d. c. 160)

Polycarp was chief pastor and bishop of the church in Smyrna and perhaps the leading Christian figure in Roman Asia in the middle of the second century. Soon after his return from a visit to Rome to confer with the church there, Polycarp was arrested during a pagan festival and since he refused to recant his faith in Christ he was burnt to death. This was on either the 23rd February 155 or the same day in 156.

Soon after the death of Polycarp and his fellow martyrs, a request reached his congregation in Smyrna for an account of the event. This came from the church at Philomelium, some two hundred miles away. Thus Marcion (we know nothing about him) who had been an eye-witness wrote the account — an account which is the earliest genuine description of a Christian martyr that we possess.

Marcion tells how the aged Polycarp was brought into the arena before the crowd and ordered by the Roman Governor to recant and to swear an oath 'By the luck of Caesar'. But Polycarp refused and instead called for the fall of paganism.

'The Governor, however, still went on pressing him. "Take the oath and I will let you go", he told him, "Revile your Christ". Polycarp's reply was, "Eighty and six years have I served him and he has done me no wrong. How can I blaspheme my King and my Saviour?" '

Still the Governor persisted and engaged in a long

conversation with Polycarp about God's government of the world and judgement of all men at the end of the age. While Polycarp was talking 'he was overflowing with courage and joy, and his whole countenance was beaming with grace.'

Meanwhile, the crowd was becoming impatient; they cried out for his death and made ready a fire on which to place him. He was tied to the stake and while his persecutors prepared to light the wood he prayed to God the Father Almighty, Father of our Lord Jesus Christ. When the fire was lit it took a strange shape. 'The fire took on the shape of a hollow chamber, like a ship's sail when the wind fills it, and formed a wall around the martyr's figure' as if he were a loaf in a baker's oven. Those present 'became aware of a delicious fragrance, like the odour of incense or other precious gums'. In fact the fire would not consume Polycarp and so one of the men rushed forward and stabbed him with a dagger.

Later, the centurion ordered the now dead body of Polycarp to be burned and the Christians were then allowed to take away his charred bones – 'more precious to us than jewels, and finer than pure gold' – for Christian burial. This is a very moving account, showing in a direct way that Christian spirituality involves giving one's all to Jesus.

63
Autobiography

GEORGE MÜLLER
(1805–1898)

Born in Prussia of Lutheran background, he went to England to study to be a missionary to Jews but instead became a member of the Open Brethren. He is chiefly remembered for the orphanage he began in 1835 in Bristol (which still exists) and for his total commitment to the principle of 'by faith alone' both for himself and for the work in which he was involved.

The *Autobiography* contains his Diary, some letters and sermons and other pieces he wrote. Here is a revealing entry for January 17, 1838, concerning his work with orphans:

The Lord is yet merciful to me. I enjoy fervency of spirit. My soul has been again repeatedly led out in prayer this day, and that for a considerable time. I have read upon my knees Psalm 60 verse 5: 'Father of the fatherless', one of the titles of Jehovah, has been a special blessing to me, with reference to the orphans. The truth, which is contained in this, I never realised so much as today. By the help of God this shall be my argument before him, respecting the orphans, in the hour of need. He is their Father, and therefore has pledged himself, as it were, to provide for them, and to care for them; and I have only to remind him of the need of these poor children, in order to have it supplied. My soul is still more enlarged respecting orphans. This word, 'a Father of the fatherless', contains enough encouragement to cast thousands of orphans upon the loving heart of God.

And this is what he did. The way the Lord supplied their needs, often at the very last minute, makes for delightful reading.

Müller had a very happy marriage: preaching the funeral sermon for his wife he told the crowd:

Our happiness in God, and in each other, was indescribable. We had not some happy days each year, nor a month of happiness each year; but we had twelve months of happiness in the year and thus year after year. Often and often I would say to my beloved one, and this again and again in the fortieth year of our conjugal union, 'My darling, do you think there is a couple in Bristol, or in the world, happier than we are?' Why do I refer to all this? To show what a remarkably great blessing to a husband is a truly godly wife, who also in other respects is fitted for him.

His account of the way in which he arose early each morning to read the Scripture, meditate upon it as if it were a letter sent down from heaven for him that very morning, and then engage in prayer as his mind and heart were moved by the meditation, is instructive. He insisted that the right way was to meditate first and then engage in petition and intercession, for the soul needed to be fed and enlarged in order rightly to engage in dialogue with God, claim his promises and make large requests of him. His example speaks to us over the years.

64

Apologia Pro Vita Sua

JOHN HENRY NEWMAN
(1801–1890)

Newman is one of the outstanding Christian figures in England in the nineteenth century. He never intended to set forth his story of how he, as a successful Oxford don and preacher, gave up everything to join the despised remnant of Roman Catholics in England. But Charles Kingsley caused him to write *An Apology for his Life* when he wrote these words in 1864 in the influential MacMillan's Magazine. 'Truth for its own sake has never been a virtue of the Roman Clergy. Father Newman informs us that it need not, and on the whole, ought not to be.' By nature Newman was a very shy and sensitive man and it was only after much heart-searching that he put on paper descriptions of his spiritual pilgrimage from an Evangelical, through a Tractarian, into a Catholic faith in search of a right relationship with God and his Church and of God's Truth as shown in Jesus Christ.

The book is written in excellent English and tells of spirituality based upon the sacred Scriptures and guided by the interpretation of the Scriptures made by the Fathers of the early centuries. From Ignatius of Antioch he learned to appreciate the Eucharist and the liturgical role of the bishop; from Athanasius he came to see the centrality of the Incarnation for life and theology; and in the development of doctrine in the Church in the first five centuries he came to see the strategic role of the Bishop of Rome. From the Fathers he came to see the great value of prayer, fasting and other disciplines of the Christian life.

His narrative of his life ends with his reception into the Catholic Church. However, the book does not stop there for he adds a series of reflections by way of a general answer to Kingsley. This part begins:

From the time that I became a Catholic . . . I have had perfect peace and contentment. I never had one doubt. I was not conscious, on my conversion, of any inward difference of thought or of temper from what I had before. I was not conscious of a firmer faith in the fundamental truths of revelation, or of more self-command; I had not more fervour; but it was like coming into port after a rough sea; and my happiness on that score remains to this day without interruption.

Nor had I any trouble about receiving those additional articles, which are not found in the Anglican Creed. Some of them I believed already, but not any one of them was a trial to me. I made profession of them upon my reception with the greatest ease, and I have the same ease in believing them now.

He went on to explain that he was sensitive to the difficulties attached to some of these articles of faith but this was no reason for doubting them.

65

Letters

JOHN NEWTON
(1725–1807)

Newton is possibly best known today as the writer of certain popular hymns – 'Amazing Grace', 'How sweet the name of Jesus sounds', and 'Glorious Things of Thee are spoken'. However, he was best known in the late eighteenth and nineteenth centuries as the letter-writer par excellence. Certainly the *Olney Hymns* (1779), which he wrote with William Cowper were popular and sung in many churches; but, it was his *Cardiphonia* (1781, many times reprinted) that people read.

This book contains a selection from his religious correspondence; it also contains what Alexander Whyte (in his preface to the 1911 edition) described as 'pure apostolical and evangelical truth, written in a strong, clear, level and idiomatic English style'. The easy and natural style of the book, its sincerity, fervour and almost womanly tenderness, together with the vivid presentation of evangelical faith and truth, gave it an immediate popularity: and it opened to Newton his most distinctive office in the Evangelical Revival – that of a writer of spiritual letters.

There are other selections of his letters. In *Omicron* (1774) and *Letters to a Wife* (2 vols 1793) are further examples of his power and tenderness as a writer to individuals of the grace of God in our Lord Jesus Christ. Those to his wife, who died of cancer in 1791 and whom he confessed to love with what he feared was an idolatrous love, are deeply touching. Though it is difficult now to get a complete edition of any of these three collections of letters, selections have been published under the title of *Letters of John Newton*. Here is what he wrote in a letter in *Cardiphonia* about submitting to the will of the Lord:

It is indeed natural for us to wish and to plan, and it is merciful in the Lord to disappoint our plans and to cross our wishes. For we cannot be safe, much less happy, but in proportion as we are weaned from our own wills and made simply desirous of being directed by his guidance. This truth (when we are enlightened by his Word) is sufficiently familiar to the judgement; but we seldom learn to reduce it into practice, without being trained awhile in the school of disappointment. The schemes we form look so plausible and convenient, that when they are broken we are ready to say, What a pity! We try again, and with no better success: we are grieved, and perhaps angry, and plan out another, and so on: at length, in the course of time, experience and observation begin to convince us, that we are not more able than we are worthy to choose aright for ourselves. Then the Lord's invitation to cast our cares upon him, and his promise to take care of us, appear valuable; and when we have done planning, his plan in our favour gradually opens, and he does more and better for us than we could either ask or think.

Though social conditions have much changed, the spiritual themes he addresses are seemingly ever with us.

66

The Vision of God

NICHOLAS OF CUSA
(1401–1464)

This book is for those who feel a need of an intellectual context
for their spirituality, even though they know that by reason
alone they cannot see or know God. Nicholas came from Cues
on the Moselle, and was a philosopher, theologian and a
cardinal. He was much involved in the ecclesiastical affairs of
his day but yet he made time to write. His major work has the
strange title, *On Learned Ignorance* (1440). He taught that God
is at once infinitely great and infinitely small, that is, he is
simultaneously the maximum and the minimum, the centre
and circumference of the universe, everywhere and nowhere,
neither only One nor only Three, but Three in One and One
in Three. The road to Truth leads beyond reason and the
principle of contradiction for.it is only by intuition that we can
'discover' God. Thus man's very knowledge of his inability
and impotence to command the whole truth about anything
and especially of God constitutes the beginning of
understanding; faith leads in this state of learned ignorance.

The Vision of God (1453) has this learned ignorance for its
intellectual background. When he sent the book to the
Benedictine monks of Tegernsee, who had requested help with
mystical theology, he sent with it an icon, the face of which
appeared to be looking in every direction. This is why the full
title of the book is *The Vision of God and the Icon*.The plan was
that the monks had the icon before them as the book was read.

There are twenty-five meditations, of which the first ten relate to the 'Face' on the icon. The next five are the most difficult for the reader since they are a review of the argument of *On Learned Ignorance* picking up points necessary to lead his reader on to contemplate the vision of God. In the final ten he meditates upon God as the Trinity and upon the union of the divine and human natures in the One Christ.

The experience of God expressed in both these books is that of ineffable, indescribable sweetness and intellectually ordered delight. Yet the contemplative dimension, which is open through Christ and reaches its heights in Christ, also becomes the active dimension with Christ in the Church and the world. Christ the Mediator unites not only God and man but also the contemplative and active lives. This is the way of faith working in and by love. And Nicholas demonstrated this happy union in his own life which was characterised by prayer and activity, contemplation and responsibility, meditation and leadership, worship and ecclesiastical order, faith and sacraments, love and good works. 'The love of your neighbour is not enough, unless it is also in God, and the existence of the sacrament is necessary for salvation, so that you may be incorporated in the unity of the body of Christ and the head of Christ, for otherwise you cannot live.'

67

Pensées

BLAISE PASCAL
(1623–1662)

Pascal is to France what Dante is to Italy and Shakespeare is to England. He inherited wealth but through his precocious and brilliant mind became a scientist as well as a man of letters. To him the Christianity of the Catholic Faith was central and he spoke of having two conversions. The first was from a nominal Christianity to a serious search for God and the taking of the sinfulness of man and the grace of God most seriously. The second conversion, when he believed that he truly was encountered by the living God, occurred on 23rd November 1654, led to his writing of his reflections about God and humanity, and was described by him in this way:

From about half past ten in the evening until about half-past twelve. FIRE. God of Abraham, God of Isaac, God of Jacob, not of the philosophers and scholars. Certitude. Certitude. Feeling. Joy. Peace. God of Jesus Christ, 'My God and your God' (Jn 20:17). Forgetfulness of the world and everything except God. He is to be found only by ways taught in the Gospel. Greatness of the human soul. 'Righteous Father the world has not known you, but I have known you'(Jn 17:25). Joy, joy, joy, tears of joy. I have separated myself from him. 'They have forsaken me, the fountain of living waters' (Jer 2:13).' My God, will you leave me?'(Matt 27:46). Let me not be separated from him eternally. 'This is eternal life that they may know you, the only true God, and the one whom you have sent, Jesus Christ' (Jn 17:3). Jesus Christ. Jesus Christ. I have separated myself from him: I have fled from him, denied him, crucified him. Let me never be separated from him. We must keep hold of him by the ways taught in the Gospel. Renunciation, total and sweet. Total submission to Jesus Christ and to my director. Eternally in joy for a day's training on earth. 'I will not forget your words' (Ps.118:16). Amen.'

Fire is of course a familiar biblical symbol for the holy yet gracious presence of God.

The Pensées take up these themes and others to insist that we can only find true happiness in life through faith and faithfulness to God, Father of our Lord Jesus Christ. They contain what has been known as 'Pascal's Wager' – God's existence cannot be proved by human thought; but, it is reasonable, however, to wager that God does truly exist. The God who does exist is not the God of the philosophers, the God subject to human reason's account of him, but the God of the patriarchs of Israel, the God of fire, revelation, grace and glory, and the God incarnate as Jesus Christ. Only this God can redeem human beings who are sinful by nature and fill their souls with his love. Thus, this is a book, not to be devoured at one sitting, but when time permits both reading and time to reflect upon the insights of Pascal.

68

On Prayer and Meditation

PETER OF ALCÁNTARA
(1499–1562)

After studying at Salamanca University in Spain, Peter joined the Franciscan Order and by 1538 had reached the rank of provincial. He founded houses where the strictest form of the Franciscan Rule was kept – the Spanish Discalced Franciscans. He is reputed to have said: 'My body and I have a compact: while I live in this world it is to suffer without intermission, but when I reach heaven I will give it eternal rest.'

His advice to lay-people on the art of prayer and meditation was set out in his *Tratado de la oracion y meditacion* (1556). Since many have felt that it is worth its weight in gold, several English translations have had the title *A Golden Treatise on Mental Prayer* (e.g. 1623, 1904, 1940). In the book Peter supplies both a method of meditation and fourteen examples of meditation.

The method of meditating upon a Scriptural text or theme is simple. First, there is spiritual preparation which includes confessing one's sins and asking for the illumination of the Holy Spirit. Secondly the passage is to be read slowly, carefully and prayerfully, noting every word, phrase and sentence, and seeing the whole as from the Lord. Thirdly, there is the actual meditation in which either the imagination or the understanding will be dominant. If the reading is from the Gospels then by the imagination one will picture the scene, listen to Jesus and appreciate with one's senses the power of his presence, words and works. If the reading is straight teaching then there will be need for the understanding to roam over and through the topic in order to digest it as a personal word from the Lord. Fourthly, having read and appropriated God's message it is right to offer thanksgiving for his grace and favour. Fifthly, in prayer one offers oneself to God, asking him to use, guide, mould and purify one's life. Finally, there is the offering to God of petitions and intercessions.

Peter explained the difference between meditation and contemplation in this way, and desired that his readers experience true contemplative prayer:

We should endeavour to unite Meditation and Contemplation, making of the first a ladder for attaining to the second . . . The very office of Meditation is to consider divine things with studiousness and attention, passing from one to another, to move our hearts to some affection and deep feeling for them, which is as though one should strike a flint to draw forth from it a spark. Contemplation is to have drawn forth this spark: I mean, to have now found this affection and feeling which were sought for, and to be in peace and silence enjoying them; not with many discursive and intellectual speculations but with a simple gaze upon the truth.

To meditate is good: to contemplate better!

69

The Twelve Patriarchs and The Mystical Ark

RICHARD OF ST VICTOR
(c. 1123–1173)

The Abbey of St Victor, home of the Augustinian Canons Regular, flourished under Hugh of St Victor, of whom Richard was an appreciative disciple. In fact Richard became sub-prior in 1159 and prior in 1162. As a theologian he is remembered for his great work, *On the Trinity*; in this is found his mystical theology which is more easily studied in *The Twelve Patriarchs and The Mystical Ark**. These have often been called *Benjamin Minor* and *Benjamin Major* respectively because Benjamin, son of Jacob, is used to personify contemplation in the first book, and by association Benjamin is also used in the related second book (which is twice the length of the first).

The first book makes great use of allegory, taking the two wives (Leah and Rachel) of Jacob to symbolize the active and contemplative aspects of the spiritual life. Benjamin, youngest of the twelve patriarchs and son of Rachel, represents contemplation, which is the crown of the virtuous life.

The second book, though longer, develops what is said about Rachel in the first, and sets forth six different modes of contemplation. Six salient features of the Ark of the Covenant (whose design God revealed to Moses)represent these six ways of contemplating God – the wood (pure imagination), the overlay of gold and the crown (two combinations of imagination and reason), the golden mercy seat (pure reason)

145

and the two golden cherubim (two stages of intellectual insight).

There is little doubt that here we have a profound analysis of the path of contemplative prayer which makes use of deep pyschological understanding. The allegorical interpretation of Scripture, at first strange, soon makes sense as the method is grasped. However, much that he says is clear and plain. For example he wrote: 'That mode of contemplation which takes place by enlarging of the mind is accustomed to increase according to three stages: by art, by exercise and by attention. We truly acquire for ourselves an art for something when we learn by accurate instruction or from wide investigation how something ought to be done. Exercise is when we put into use what we have received by means of art and make ourselves ready and prepared for carrying out such a function. Attention is when we pursue with zeal what we have accomplished with the greatest care. . . . And so by these three stages the inner recess of the mind is enlarged and made more capable for any learning and skill.' With the enlarging of the mind by divine truth there also comes delight in God, delight which, as contemplation is intensified and enriched becomes ecstasy.

These two books are for those who seriously want to discover a way of contemplative prayer which was regarded in medieval times as belonging to the highest calling of human beings in their service of God.

70

The Fire of Love

RICHARD ROLLE
(c.1300–1349)

Born in Thorton-le-Dale in Yorkshire, he studied at Oxford and
then returned to the North of England. He became a hermit
and eventually the spiritual director of the Cistercian nuns at
Hampole, near Doncaster. He was the author of a rich and
varied body of writings both in Latin and English and often
highly alliterative. The *Fire of Love* was written in 1343 and is
his best known work.The book is really a series of discourses
on topics related to the life of a hermit. In the prologue Rolle
expresses his conviction that the life he has chosen brings real
joy; the next eleven chapters are devoted to what is involved
in embarking upon the life of a solitary. The next two chapters
provide autobiography rather than advice, while the remaining
chapters deal with various difficulties of the life of the hermit
devoted to contemplative prayer.

The opening words of the Prologue provide the key to the
title of the book. Rolle explains:

> I cannot tell you how surprised I was the first time I felt my
> heart begin to warm. It was real warmth too, not imaginary,
> and it felt as if it were actually on fire. I was astonished at
> the way the heat surged up, and how this new sensation
> brought great and unexpected comfort. I had to keep feeling
> my breast to make sure there was no physical reason for it!
> But once I realised that it came entirely from within, that this

fire of love had no cause – material or sinful – but was the gift of my Maker, I was absolutely delighted, and wanted my love to be even greater.

In the book he has much to say about the love of the soul for God, offered in response to God's initiative of love. 'The love to which we are rising by this work (of contemplative prayer) is hotter than any burning coal and will undoubtedly leave its mark on us, because it will make our spirits glowing and splendid.' This fire of love is the very love 'which lays hold of Christ and brings him into our hearts; which sweetens our minds so that in our hearts we burst out singing our hymns of praise, rejoicing in spiritual music'. Rolle believed that there is no pleasure to compare with this 'which intoxicates with genuine sweetness and delights with holy charm'. For the soul which receives it is purged by sacred fire and nothing remains in it of decay or darkness.

Rolle confessed that:

Love is the sweetest and most useful thing a rational creature can ever acquire. Most acceptable and pleasing to God, it not only binds the soul with bands of wisdom and sweetness when it joins it to God, but it also remains flesh and blood, so that a man does not go after mistaken delights, or wander off in search of error of various kinds. Through love of this kind the heart grows healthy and our life finds meaning and strength. Little wonder then that I never found a better or sweeter dwelling-place. For love unites me, love and me, and makes of two one.

Reading his book will warm your heart!

71

The Life, Walk and Triumph of Faith

WILLIAM ROMAINE
(1714–1795)

Romaine was one of the leaders of the Evangelical Revival of
the eighteenth century who remained a parish minister and
did not travel from place to place like the Wesley brothers.
From 1766 he was Rector of St Anne's, Blackfriars, London.
His trilogy came out in stages between 1771 and 1794 and since
that date has been published as a whole.

The text is dense with scriptural quotation and allusion but
the meaning is very clear. The Christian life is presented as
being by grace through faith; union with Christ is by the Spirit
in faith; it may also be said to be a humble trusting in God
the Father while walking in and with Christ. There is before
the believer the hope that he will see his Lord and his faith
will triumph as he delights in the love and glory of God in
heaven. He will therefore pray often in words like these:

Let me see thee face to face, and enjoy thee, thou dearest
Jesus, whom my soul longeth after. It is good to live upon
thee by faith, but to live with thee is best of all. I have found
one day in thy courts, conversing sweetly with thee, better
than a thousand, but this has only whetted my appetite; the
more communion I have with thee, I hunger and thirst still
for more. My soul panteth for nearer, still nearer communion
with thee. When shall I come to appear before the presence
of God? O thou light of my life, thou joy of my heart, thou

knowest how I wish for the end of my faith, when I shall no longer see through a glass darkly, but with open face behold the glory of my Lord . . . Come, Lord Jesus, let me see thee as thou art. Come, and make me like unto thee. I do love thee; I am now happy in thy love, but not so as I hope to be . . . Even so, come Lord Jesus.

Romaine expected that such breathings of the soul would occur in all who were truly living and walking by faith. Consciousness of belonging to the supernatural world – the commonwealth of heaven where Christ reigns as Lord – is basic to his spirituality and piety.

One of the attractive features of this trilogy is that Romaine moves from explaining such high matters as the doctrine of the Trinity into a meditation upon the grace of God, Father, Son and Holy Spirit and then into a prayer – a prayer which has all the marks of having been first prayed by himself for himself. Doctrine is practical and holiness is doctrinal. Faith is trusting and believing; but the God who is trusted and the promises which are believed have content which is to be received and meditated upon. Illustrations are few but the content is clear; however, because Romaine is so deeply immersed in Scripture and reflects this even when he is not directly quoting from it, he is best appreciated by those who have a good working knowledge of the contents of the Bible.

See my biography of Romaine in the 1970 edition of this trilogy (James Clarke).

72

Letters

SAMUEL RUTHERFORD
(1600–1661)

As the minister of Anwoth in Kirkcudbrightshire in Scotland he gave himself unreservedly to the pastoral ministry, holding his parishioners spellbound by his descriptions of the loveliness of Christ. Here his ministry was most fruitful from 1627 until 1636 when he was deposed from office because of nonconformity and confined in Aberdeen prison during the King's pleasure. It was from here that he wrote letters to his former flock and it is these letters, as collected by Andrew Bonar, which have been regarded both in Scotland and elsewhere as a treasury of devotion. He was released from prison in 1638 and after a brief period back at Anwoth became professor of divinity at St Andrews.

To William Gordon, Rutherford wrote about wasted opportunities in life to grow in the grace and knowledge of our Lord: 'Alas! that the sharp and bitter blasts on face and sides, which meet us in this life, have not learned us mortification, and made us dead to this world. We buy our own sorrow, and we pay dear for it, when we spend our love, our joy, our desires, our confidence upon an handful of snow and ice, that time will melt away to nothing, and go thirsty out of the drunken inn when all is done.' Then he proceeded to speak of Christ:

I know no wholesome fountain but one. I know not a thing

worth the buying but heaven; and my own mind is, if comparison were made betwixt Christ and heaven, I would fell heaven with my blessing and buy Christ. O if I could raise the market for Christ, and heighten the market a pound for a penny, and cry up Christ in men's estimation ten thousand talents more than men think of him! But they are shaping him, and crying him down, and valuing him at their unworthy halfpenny; or else exchanging and bartering Christ with the miserable old fallen house of this vain world. Or if they do not do this they lend him out upon interest and play the usurers with Christ: because they profess him and give out before men that Christ is their treasure and stock; and, in the mean time, praise of men, and a name, and ease, and the summer sun of the Gospel, is the usury they would be at. Happy are they who can keep Christ by himself alone, and keep him clean and whole, till God come and count with them.

The letter closes with further reflections on the place of suffering in the Christian life.

The three hundred and sixty-five letters reflect a deep personal and affectionate love for Jesus in this pastor's heart and those who read them cannot but be profoundly moved. The well-known hymn, 'The sands of time are sinking, The dawn of heaven breaks . . .' is a skilful mosaic of phrases from Rutherford's *Letters* and *Dying Sayings* by Anne Ross Cousin. Reading the full nineteen verses of this hymn is a good way to get a feel for the spirituality of Rutherford.

73

The Sparkling Stone

JAN VAN RUYSBROECK
(1293–1381)

Born at Brabant in the Low Countries, he was ordained as a priest when twenty-four years old and then was attached to the collegiate church of St Gudule in Brussels for twenty-five years. In 1343 he retired to a hermitage at Groenendael in the forest of Soignes with two companions. Six years later this group became a community of Augustinian Canons Regular. In this quiet setting Ruysbroeck was able to do much writing, of which *The Sparkling Stone* is one of the most accessible to the beginner in mystical literature.

The theological foundation of the spirituality of Ruysbroeck is the doctrine of the Trinity. As in breathing where there is inhaling and exhaling so in the spiritual life there is aspiration and expiration: that is, God draws the contemplative to himself and then, in and by the Holy Spirit (the Breath of God) sends him back into the world for the practice of good works to the glory of God.

Ruysbroeck explained that

the man who is sent down by God from these heights (of mystical union in contemplation) into the world is full of truth and rich in the virtues. And he seeks not his own but the glory of him who has sent him. And hence he is just and truthful in all things, and he possesses a rich and generous foundation which rests in the riches of God, and therefore

153

he must always spend himself on those who have need of him; for the living fount of the Holy Spirit which is his wealth can never be spent . . . He stands ready and willing to do all that God commands and is strong and courageous in suffering and enduring all that God sends him. He therefore leads a universal (common) life for he is equally ready for contemplation or for action and is perfect at both.

Therefore the contemplative and active aspects of the Christian life belong together − but only on the basis that the contemplative has the priority for there is the going to God before being sent by him into his world.

The Sparkling Stone has its origin in Revelation 2:17 where Christ promises to give a stone with a new name written on it to the faithful Christians of Pergamum. 'This stone is shining white and red like a flame of fire; and it is small and round and smooth all over, and very light. By this sparkling stone we mean our Lord Jesus Christ, for he is, according to his Godhead, a shining forth of Eternal Light, and an irradiation of the glory of God, and a flawless mirror in which all things have their life . . .' To the one who overcomes the world, the flesh and the devil is this Stone given and with it come light and truth and life. The new name written on it is the 'secret name' given by God to the soul in the heights of contemplation.

74

Holiness

JOHN CHARLES RYLE
(1816–1900)

Ryle was a leader of Evangelicals in the Church of England and became the first Bishop of Liverpool in 1880. He employed his intellectual ability to write about scriptural Christianity and aspects of Church history in a simple and attractive manner for ordinary people. In fact as a young incumbent he worked hard to develop a simple and clear literary style. He was thoroughly committed to the Church of England, its Liturgy and the Thirty-Nine Articles of Religion.

The full title of this book was *Holiness: its nature, hindrances, difficulties and roots.* It has been regularly reprinted since it first appeared in 1877. In introducing the twenty papers which make up the book he wrote:

I have had a deep conviction for many years that practical holiness and entire self-consecration to God are not sufficiently attended to by modern Christians in this country. Politics, or controversy, or party-spirit, or worldliness, have eaten out the heart of piety in many of us. The subject of personal godliness has fallen sadly into the background. The standard of living has become painfully low in many quarters. The immense importance of 'adorning the doctrine of God our Saviour' (Titus 2:10), and making it lovely and beautiful by our daily habits and characters, has been far too much overlooked.

Then, speaking as a convinced evangelical churchman he said:

> Sound Protestant and Evangelical doctrine is useless if it is
> not accompanied by a holy life. It is worse than useless; it
> does positive harm. It is despised by keen-sighted and
> shrewd men of the world, as an unreal and hollow thing,
> and brings religion into contempt. It is my firm impression
> that we want a thorough revival about scriptural holiness . . .

Some would want to say the same in the late twentieth century!

The subject matter of the book is warm, evangelical,
scriptural, and attractive. He explained that holiness includes
all these elements – the habit of being of one mind with God,
loving what he loves; the endeavour to shun every known sin
and keep every known commandment; the striving to be like
our Lord Jesus Christ; the following after meekness,
longsuffering, gentleness, patience, temperance and self-denial
as well as charity and brotherly kindness; the possession of
a spirit of mercy and benevolence towards others; the desire
for purity of heart and spiritual mindedness as well as a true
reverence/fear of God; and a faithfulness in all the duties and
relations in life.

75

Pia Desideria

PHILIP JACOB SPENER
(1635–1705)

The publication in 1675 at Frankfurt of *Pia Desideria* (Pious Wishes), which is a 'heartfelt desire for God-pleasing reform' of the Church was a major factor in the rise of the renewal movement called Pietism. Spener was influenced early in life by Johann Arndt's *True Christianity* (see p.15) as well as by the writings of English Puritans. He became a Lutheran pastor and was at Frankfurt from 1666. Here apart from the ministry of the Word and the Sacrament he introduced fellowship meetings (Collegia Pietatis) in his home. Also he took the opportunity offered by a local publisher to write a foreword to a book of Arndt's sermons. This preface caused such a sensation that he published it separately in a longer form as *Pia Desideria*.

The book has three parts. The first reviews the shortcomings of the Church at that time – sin was not taken seriously and religious duties were performed in superficial ways. The second part proposes that there is a possibility of reform and there is no need for despair. The promises of God in Scripture and the example of the early Church offer great encouragement! In the final part six proposals are offered for making reform and renewal possible: (1) Much greater use of the sacred Scriptures. (2) More involvement by laity in the life of the Church. (3) Encouragement of the practical as well as the intellectual aspects of the faith – especially the spirit of love in action. (4) Charity exercised in religious controversy. (5) Educating ministers in a way that combines piety and learning. (6) Preaching which edifies and renews as well as informs.

To illustrate his general style and approach here is part of what he writes under the fifth proposal:

> Since ministers must bear the greatest burden in all these things which pertain to reform of the Church, and since their shortcomings do correspondingly great(er) harm, it is of the utmost importance that the office of the ministry be occupied by men who, above all, are themselves true Christians and, then, have the divine wisdom to guide others carefully on the way of the Lord. It is therefore important, indeed necessary, for the reform of the Church that only such persons be called who may be suited, and that nothing at all except the glory of God be kept in view during the whole procedure of calling. This would mean that all carnal schemes involving favour, friendship, gifts, and similarly unseemly things would be set aside. Not the last among the reasons for the defect in the Church are all the mistakes which occur in the calling of ministers, but we shall not elaborate on that here.

Later he adds these important words on preaching: 'Our whole Christian religion consists of the inner man or the new man, whose soul is faith and whose expressions are the fruits of life and all sermons should be aimed at this.'

76

Autobiography

CHARLES HADDON SPURGEON
(1834–1892)

Spurgeon was a man of many parts but he is remembered primarily as the great preacher who was heard by thousands each week in London and whose printed sermons were read by many more thousands. He also founded a theological college, established an orphanage, wrote books on preaching and the ministry, produced devotional books (e.g. *Morning and Evening*) and the monumental commentary on the Psalter entitled *The Treasury of David* (a truly great book in six volumes). His spirituality was rooted in the teaching of the English Puritans, whom he loved to read, as well as in that of the Calvinist leaders of the Evangelical Revival whose labours inspired him. He desired to be an evangelist and a pastor, a soul-winner and a soul physician, a godly and learned preacher and a faithful and devoted husband and father.

His evangelical piety, deeply rooted in a Calvinist view of the sovereignty of the God of all grace and mercy and the pre-eminence of Jesus Christ, is apparent in all his writings. However, in his extensive autobiography it is found rooted in the rough and tumble of life, which included a fair share of suffering and pain. His son wrote: 'I know of no one who could, more sweetly than my dear father, impart comfort to bleeding hearts and sad spirits. As the crushing of the flower causes it to yield its aroma, so he, having endured in the long-continued suffering of my beloved mother, and also constant pains in himself, was able to sympathize most tenderly with all sufferers.' Thus the great preacher had also the great gift of sympathy.

In the winter of 1887 – 8 after several months of both physical illness and heartache, he told of what the furnace of affliction had done for him:

To the cheering Scriptures, I have added testimonies of my own, the fruit of trial and experience. I believe all the promises of God, but many of them I have personally tried and proved . . . I have been cast into 'waters to swim in' which, but for God's upholding hand, would have proved waters to drown in . . . I do not mention this to exact sympathy, but simply to let you see that I am no dry-land sailor. I have traversed these oceans which are not Pacific full many a time: I know the roll of the billows, and the rush of the winds. Never were the promises of Jehovah so precious to me as at this hour. Some of them I never understood till now; I had not reached the date at which they matured, for I was not myself mature enough to perceive their meaning. How much more wonderful is the Bible to me now than it was a few months ago. In obeying the Lord, and bearing his reproach outside the camp, I have not received new promises; but the result to me is much he same as if I had done so, for the old ones have opened up to me with richer stores.

The pastor who learns in this way has truly a message to share!

77

At the Feet of the Master

SADHU SUNDAR SINGH
(1889–1929)

Born into a wealthy home at Rampur in North Punjab, India, in 1889 Sundar Singh was educated at a Presbyterian Mission School. Later, to show his opposition to Christianity he publicly burned a copy of the Christian Bible in the courtyard of his father's house. Three days later he had a vision of Jesus Christ and to the great surprise and horror of his family immediately became a Christian. He described it in these words: 'As I prayed and looked into the light, I saw the form of the Lord Jesus Christ. It had such an appearance of glory and love! – I heard a voice saying in Hindustani, "How long will you persecute me? I have come to save you." So I fell at his feet and got a wonderful peace . . . This was heaven itself.' After this vision he spent many days in solitude, engaged in prayer. During this time he received a deep sense of God's forgiveness together with a commission from his Saviour to go forth and tell the good news.

The result was that he was driven out of the family home for betraying the Sikh religion. He became a Sadhu, a holy man without possessions dressed in a simple saffron robe and going from place to place to preach Christ. His life story is a fascinating combination of evangelistic zeal, gospel poverty and visions given to him as he spent long hours in meditation, contemplation and prayer.

This little book contains a record of dialogue which took place

161

between the Lord Jesus and his Sadhu. They explore the mystery of pain, suffering and sin. A friend commented:

> Closely akin to his love of solitude (he would spend whole days or nights in a cave) I would place his great passion for the supernatural world in which alone he could find peace. This explains, as nothing else can do, many of his actions. It would lead him, for instance, to spend the whole night in prayer, in some solitary place, or on some lonely mountain. We would see him when he returned and there would be a serenity about him which was visible to us all. He would speak very little of what he had experienced, but his face itself would tell us what he himself did not reveal.

He had received the gift of ecstasy in prayer and in his simple lifestyle he valued this more than everything money could buy. 'The Presence of Christ, which the eyes of the mind make real to us, is no mere fancy', he would say, 'it is the greatest reality in the inner world of spirit today, without which human life would be impossible of fullness.'

The value of this book, translated from Urdu in 1927, is that it presents us with a genuinely Eastern Christian spirituality and shows how deep, mystical prayer and the active life of preaching the Gospel belong together. There is perhaps a timely message here in days when some Christians are seeking to find God through Hindu or Buddhist spirituality. There are good biographies of Sundar Singh by Mrs Parker and C.F. Andrews.

78

The Little Book of Eternal Wisdom

HEINRICH SUSO
(c.1295–1366)

As a monk, Suso spent much of his ministry (1347–1366) at the Dominican monastery at Ulm on the Danube. It was here that he had the leisure to collect his writings together and produce new ones. Before this, he had studied under Meister Eckhart at Cologne and had gained a deep admiration for his mystical theology. He had also preached in Switzerland and the Upper Rhine area where he was a highly valued spiritual director in the convents of the Dominican Order.

His principal work, *The Little Book of Eternal Wisdom*, originally composed in 1328 is a practical meditation book with very little theory. It concludes with a hundred brief meditations on the Passion. The text makes for easy reading because it is in the form of a series of conversations between the Servant (Suso) and Eternal Wisdom (Christ). Apart from the actual teaching which is contained in these, there are many insights provided into the spiritual experience of Suso himself (experiences which may be supplemented by reading his *Life* and his *Little Book of Truth*).

Eternal Wisdom makes clear to the Servant that the way to please God and enjoy the sweet pleasure of communion with him is only possible by one way: 'No one can attain to divine heights or to unusual sweetness unless he be first drawn through the example of my human bitterness. The higher one climbs without passing through my humanity, the deeper one

163

falls. My humanity is the way by which one must go; sufferings are the gate through which one must pass.' And, in response to the hesitations of the Servant and his further questions, Eternal Wisdom speaks once more of the necessity of imitating him: 'Be not afraid of imitating my sufferings. For if God is so fully within a man that suffering becomes easy for him, then he has no cause for complaint. No one enjoys my presence more in unusual sweetness than those who share with me the hardest bitterness. No one complains more about the bitterness of the husk than he who knows not the sweetness of the kernel.'

Suso insists that entire self-surrender to God is the only way to true union with God. To imitate Jesus means to 'Break your pleasure in frivolous seeing and idle hearing; let love taste good to you and take pleasure in what has been distasteful to you. You shall seek all your rest in me, love bodily discomfort, suffer evil willingly, desire contempt, renounce your desires, and die to all your lusts. That is the beginning of the school of Wisdom, which is to be read in the open and wounded book of my crucified body. And ponder this, even if man does all in his power, can anyone in the whole world do for me what I have done for him?'

79

The Discourses

SYMEON, THE NEW THEOLOGIAN
(949–1022)

Symeon was abbot of St Mamas when he wrote these thirty-four discourses. The title 'New Theologian' implies a comparison with Gregory of Nazianzus, known in the East as 'The Theologian'. He is recognized as the greatest of the Byzantine mystical writers, having a vivid and highly personal style.

The discourses originated in addresses he gave to the monks at Mattins. His personality is everywhere evident as he shares what is in his heart with his brothers. The themes to which he often turns are those found in the tradition of the spirituality of Eastern Christianity – repentance, detachment, renunciation, works of mercy, keeping God's commandments, sorrow for sins, awareness of death, purity of heart, faith and contemplation. Yet he also insists, and here he will ring bells for modern Christians in the Charismatic Movement, on the presence, power, inspiration and guidance of the Holy Spirit who leads to deeper spirituality and to the mystical union with God, the indwelling Trinity. He speaks of the Baptism in the Holy Spirit as a deeper experience of the Spirit than that given by God in association with water baptism.

Symeon is much attracted by the theme of light – God in Christ as light entering the human soul:

The light shines on us without evening, without change,

without alteration, without form. It speaks, works, lives, gives life, and changes into light those whom it illuminates. We bear witness that God is light and those to whom it has been granted to see him all have beheld him as light. Those who have received him have received him as light, because the light of his glory goes before him and it is impossible for him to appear without light. Those who have not seen his light have not seen him, for he is the light, and those who have not received the light have not yet received grace.

This light is not merely the illumination of the mind and heart; it is rather an inner, spiritual light given only to those who seek God through purity of heart.

Another theme in Symeon is the gift of tears. When a person is truly sorrowing for sin, being purified by the Spirit, and baptised in the Spirit, then the Spirit will give this gift – tears in great effusion and abundance! 'As food and drink are necessary for the body, so are tears for the soul – so much so that he who does not daily weep will destroy his soul and cause it to perish from hunger' said Symeon. In fact, 'Take away the tears and you remove with them purification', he insisted.

These discourses are not only easy to read, they are also fascinating. They provide an excellent introduction to Eastern Christian mysticism. If you like poetry read also his *Hymns of Divine Love*, translated by G.A. Maloney S.J.

80

Sermons

JOHANNES TAULER
(c.1300–1361)

First in German, then in Latin, and finally in various European languages, the Sermons of this Dominican preacher and spiritual director were published as soon as the printing presses began to function. Martin Luther got a copy of the German edition of 1505 and of Tauler remarked: 'I have found more true theology in him than in all the doctors of all the universities.' The preface to the Latin translation of 1548 – the edition which did most to establish Tauler's reputation amongst Catholics, apologised for the Protestant Luther's commendation!

Born in Strasbourg, Tauler went through the usual training as a Dominican before beginning his ministry of preaching, addressed to the large convents of Dominican nuns in Germany as well as to laypeople. His attraction as a preacher – and as the author of written sermons – seems to be in his tireless and hearty encouragement to everyone to love God and one's neighbour, to eradicate vice and pursue virtue, to be attentive to the interior life of the soul, to deny self-will and inordinate desires, to imitate Christ by meditating upon his life, to take up the Cross and suffer for Jesus, to follow him humbly and faithfully whatever the cost and wherever he leads, and to aim to be so united with God in spirit and in truth that to love him and one's neighbour in him occurs habitually.

While he emphasises that the only way to 'ascend' to God

is through the 'descent' of union with and imitation of Jesus, especially in his passion, he also speaks of this imitation resulting in the highest contemplative union with God possible here on earth:

Now I will speak of another love, and it is as high above the first as heaven is above the earth. It was experienced by the apostles after the Ascension . . . Here the self is left far behind; and instead of fullness there is emptiness. Not knowledge, but non-knowledge prevails now; for that love is beyond all modes and manners. Oh what great pain this causes our poor human nature, which is now twisting and turning like a child deprived of its mother's breast. Angry nature with its nooks and corners is totally lost because this new love transcends its power and effectiveness. So entirely stripped must it be of self that this very self eludes its glance. Neither thought nor desire can it harbour. It cannot even sacrifice this poverty to God for in its non-knowledge it cleaves closely to it. It must deny its very self, and die to all sensible images which it possessed in the first stage, in order to enter that realm where God loves himself and is his own object of love. In this denuding of ourselves we are reformed in the form of God, clothed with his divinity.

This is the stage of prayer where the human spirit rests in God's Spirit 'in the secret silence of the divine Essence'.

81

Hudson Taylor

DR AND MRS HOWARD TAYLOR
(1864–1928)

This great story of a pioneer missionary, founder of the China Inland Mission (The Overseas Missionary Fellowship), is also the story of a practical spirituality, characterised by humble trust, large vision, unswerving obedience and great courage. There are two volumes, the first with the subtitle, *The Growth of a Soul* and the second, *The Growth of a Work of God*. They were first published separately in 1911 and 1918 but since 1965 have been available as one large volume. Though there are other biographies of J. Hudson Taylor (1832–1905), it is this which deserves to be called a classic because it is written in the same spirit which motivated James Hudson Taylor himself – a simple, attractive evangelical faith which took God at his word, without fuss or bother.

He was a Yorkshire lad from a Methodist home. At seventeen he experienced a deep conversion followed by a call to go to China. He went there first in 1854, was invalided back to England, and wanted to return when China was opened up to Westerners. But no missionary society would take him and so he founded The China Inland Mission and sailed to China in 1866. From then his story is one of great faith and courage but not without suffering and pain. By 1895 he led 641 missionaries, about half the missionary force in the whole of China! He emphasised the principle of living as the Chinese did, eating and dressing as they did, and insisted that the work be guided from the place of mission not some London office. Further he insisted on the principle of living by faith – of telling God of our needs and allowing him to supply them. This aspect of his life and work is firmly embedded in a spirituality which takes as wholly true the promises of God for supplying all our needs in Christ Jesus. To it is added a mystical aspect – see his *Union and Communion: Thoughts on the Song of Solomon*.

Here is a typical statement from Hudson Taylor, reflecting his missionary spirituality:

There is a needs-be for us to give ourselves for the life of the world as Jesus gave his flesh for the feeding of the lifeless and of living souls whose life can only be nourished by the same life-giving Bread. An easy-going, non-self-denying life will never be one of power.

Fruit-bearing involves cross-bearing . . . We know how the Lord Jesus became fruitful – not by bearing his Cross merely, but by dying on it. Do we know much of fellowship with him in this? There are not two Christs – an easy-going-one for easy-going Christians, and a suffering, toiling one for exceptional believers. There is only one Christ. Are you willing to abide in him and thus to bear much fruit?

Would that God would make hell so real to us that we cannot rest; heaven so real that we must have men there; Christ so real that our supreme motive and aim shall be to make the Man of Sorrows the Man of Joy by the conversion to him of many . . .

He longed to see people converted to Jesus Christ, and was prepared to give his all to achieve this.

82

Way of Perfection

TERESA OF AVILA
(1515–1582)

Among all the saints of the Roman Catholic Church none is more greatly respected and loved as a teacher of genuine spirituality than Teresa (Teresa de Cepeda y Ahumada) who was born in Avila and entered the Carmelite Convent of the Incarnation there in 1535.

She wrote the *Way of Perfection* when she had reached the age of fifty and was then the prioress of one of the twenty convents she had founded. Although written for her nuns this is probably the most valuable and helpful of her writings to put into the hands of a modern Christian who is beginning the reading of Teresa's works. Reading this can be followed by her *Life* and *Interior Castle*.

The way to perfection is the way of loving God with heart, soul, mind and strength, of loving one's neighbour in the love of God and as one loves self, of genuine humility and detachment from personal satisfaction. Prayer is, of course, central to this way and a large part of the book is about prayer – mental prayer (meditation), vocal prayer (especially in the use of 'Our Father . . .'), the Prayer of Recollection (i.e. the prayer of acquired recollection or the prayer of simplicity – also known as the prayer of simple gaze or the simple vision of faith) and the Prayer of Quiet (mystical prayer in which the intimate awareness of God's presence captivates the will and fills the soul and body with ineffable delight.

One leads on to the other, as she explained. 'When I say the Creed, it seems to me right, and indeed obligatory, that I should understand and know what it is that I believe; and, when I repeat the "Our Father", my love should make me want to understand who this Father of ours is and who the Master is that taught us this prayer.' The mind, the affections and the will are thus drawn towards God and the path of prayer becomes a route to gaze upon God in his beauty.

On true humility in prayer she commented:

Avoid being bashful with God, as some people are, in the belief that they are being humble. It would not be humility on your part if the King were to do you a favour and you refused to accept it; but you would be showing humility by taking it, and being pleased with it, yet realizing how far you are from deserving it. A fine humility it would be if I had the Emperor of heaven and earth in my house, coming to it to do me a favour and to delight in my company, and I were so humble that I would not answer his questions, nor remain with him, nor accept what he gave me, but left him alone. Or if he were to speak to me and beg me to ask for what I wanted, and I were so humble that I preferred to remain poor and even let him go away so that he would see that I had not sufficient resolution.

Such an attitude is not true humility. Rather 'speak with him as with a Father, a Brother, a Lord and a Spouse – and sometimes in one way and sometime in another. He will teach you what you must do to please him.'

83

Life

TERESA OF AVILA
(1515–1582)

This fascinating book has for its full title: *The Life of the Holy Mother, Teresa of Jesus, and some of the favours granted to her by God, described by herself at the command of her confessor, to whom she submits and addresses it as follows.* She completed it when she was fifty, but it was not released until 1568 when her bishop finally approved it.

The way to becoming a saint (she was declared such by the Pope in 1622) and to a doctor of theology (she was made such in 1970, one of only two women having this title) is the way from sin to holiness through pain and suffering. It is costly – at least to self-interest and pride – yet it brings joys, the like of which earthly joys cannot begin to equal.

In chapter 9 she describes the means by which the Lord began to waken her and to give her light in her internal darkness. She had been a nun for nearly twenty years and in that time, perhaps due to poor spiritual direction, had not found that internal peace for which she longed:

Entering the oratory one day, I saw an image which had been procured for a certain festival . . . It represented Christ sorely wounded and so conducive was it to devotion that when I looked at it I was deeply moved to see him thus, so well did it picture what he suffered for us. So great was my distress when I thought how ill I had repaid him for those wounds that I felt as if my heart were breaking, and I threw myself down beside him, shedding floods of tears and begging him to give me strength once for all so that I might not offend him.

From this time forward she began to improve and she was further helped by the reading of Augustine's Confessions and particularly of the account of his conversion, which reduced her to more tears but also to more light.

In later chapters she shares with her readers some of her experience of communion with the Lord in prayer. For example she tells of what often happened when she made mental pictures of Christ:

I used unexpectedly to experience a consciousness of the presence of God, of such a kind that I could not possibly doubt that he was within me or that I was wholly engulfed in him. This was in some sense a vision: I believe it is called mystical theology. The soul is suspended in such a way that it seems to be completely outside itself. The will loves; the memory, I think, is almost lost; while the understanding, I believe, though it is not lost, does not reason — I mean that it does not work, but is amazed at the extent of all it can understand; for God wills it to realize that it understands nothing of what his Majesty represents to it.

The book is a unique description of her prayer-life from the darkness she experienced in using traditional methods of meditation to the mystical elation and union with God.

84

The Mansions of the Interior Castle

TERESA OF AVILA
(1515–1582)

At the age of sixty-two Teresa wrote this book, chiefly because her *Life* was in the hands of the Inquisition in Spain and people were forbidden to read it. She explained the teaching on prayer and communion with God which is set out in an autobiographical form in her *Life* in an orderly – yet natural and flexible – form. The result is a masterpiece, a mature statement of her teaching , which has profoundly influenced many women and men since its publication.

After a brief preface, she begins her theme and applies the image of a castle to the life of prayer (which is also the life of virtue, for with her the two go together). 'I began to think of the soul as if it were a castle made of a single diamond or of a very clear crystal, in which there are many rooms, just as in heaven there are many mansions.' The image is used to describe the whole course of the mystical life, that is the soul's progress from the first set of mansions to the seventh and its transformation by the grace of God from an imperfect and sinful creature into the bride of Christ in the spiritual marriage.

The first mansions (the plural is important) are the place where humility is learned; the second that of beginning to pray seriously and meditate sincerely; the third the recognising that love of God has to be the source of the moral and religious life; the fourth the movement from ordinary to contemplative prayer, where the communion with God is becoming more real; the fifth the state where the soul is inactive as it is overwhelmed with the presence and love of God, and it is here that she provides the beautiful picture of the soul as a silkworm emerging from its cocoon as a white butterfly; the sixth the spiritual betrothal where there is intimate spiritual communion between the soul and God, and this leads on to the last which may be called spiritual marriage, which is the deepest or highest union with God possible for a mortal on this earth.

Teresa's preference for the plural is to be seen as indicating that there are many possible interpretations of the development of the spiritual life in its various stages. In each mansion, she wrote, 'there are comprised many more, above and below and around, with lovely gardens and fountains, and things so delectable that you will want to lose yourselves in praise of the great God' who made the soul in his image and likeness.

This book also contains a treasury of unforgettable maxims on such themes as self-knowledge, humility, detachment and suffering. Teresa does not separate praying from being holy and behaving lovingly. She sees a unity in the contemplative and active aspects of the Christian life.

85

Autobiography

THÉRÈSE OF LISIEUX
(1873–1897)

Entering the Carmelite Monastery when only fifteen Thérèse received the religious name of Sister Thérèse of the Child Jesus and the Holy Face. When she knew she would soon die, and following the custom of the Carmelites, she wrote her autobiography which is really in three different parts – one addressed to Mother Agnes, prioress from 1893–1896, another to her successor as Prioress, Mother Marie de Gonzagne, and the third to Sister Marie of the Sacred Heart. These are usually printed together as *The Story of a Soul: The Autobiography*. From this we learn about her simple spirituality immediately before she entered Carmel. Recalling her visit to Rome, which included an audience with Leo XIII, she described her relationship to Jesus:

> I had offered myself, for some time now, to the Child Jesus as his little plaything. I told him not to use me as a valuable toy children are content to look at but dare not touch; but to use me like a little ball of no value which he could throw on the ground, push with his foot, pierce, leave in a corner, or press to his heart if it pleased him; in a word, I wanted to amuse little Jesus, to give him pleasure; I wanted to play up to his childish whims. He heard my prayer.

After she became a nun she did not lose this devotion to the

Child Jesus which in turn points to her way of confidence and abandonment to God. She expected everything from her heavenly Father; she worried about nothing for she believed he was in charge; she did not praise herself but attributed all good to him and she was not discouraged by her faults, always learning like a child.

After her full profession, a day she called the 'beautiful day of my wedding', she was aware constantly of the presence of God. She expressed it in this way:

> I understand and I know from experience that 'the kingdom of heaven is within you.' Jesus has no need of books or teachers to instruct souls. He teaches without the noise of words. Never have I heard him speak, but I feel that he is within me at each moment: he is guiding and inspiring me with what I must say and do. I find just when I need them certain lights which I had not seen until then, and it isn't most frequently during my hours of prayer that these are most abundant but in the midst of my daily occupations.

Hers was the 'Little Way' which opened the road to God for innumerable, ordinary people. She was canonized in 1925.

Her message is total oblation but in the little things of ordinary, daily life. Motive, intention, the inner direction are very important, more important than the actual doing of anything.

86

The Imitation of Christ

THOMAS À KEMPIS
(c. 1380–1471)

This book has been one of the most famous and favourite of all devotional literature. This is partly because of its clarity of style and its psychological insights and perceptiveness. The imitation is of the Lord Jesus Christ in his life of humility, love, suffering, and total and joyful submission to the Father in heaven. Though this may seem highly individualistic it does presume the reality of the fellowship of the monastery or the church. Thomas of Hamerkin of Kempen, a village near Cologne, became an Augustinian monk, at the Agnietenberg house (near Zwolle) of which his elder brother was prior. He remained there all his life, copying manuscripts and doing his own writing. He left behind a large collection of works which commend the spiritual life.

The contents of the *Imitation* are arranged in four books: the first offers general advice as to what is necessary for a spiritual life with growth in self-knowledge and growing detachment from worldly values; the second provides further advice specifically on the inner life as the way of the Cross; in the third, which is the longest, the material is about inward consolation being rooted and grounded in God alone and there are dialogues between the living Christ and his disciple; finally, in the fourth the theme is the sacrament of Holy Communion, and how rightly to receive it. For Thomas the Bible on the one side and the Lord's Supper on the other are the two great treasuries of holy mother Church.

To imitate Christ it is necessary first of all to meditate upon the account of Christ in the Gospels: 'Let our chiefest endeavour be to meditate upon the life of Jesus Christ'. 'What will it profit you to dispute profoundly on the Holy Trinity if you are devoid of humility and are thereby displeasing to God, the Trinity?' It is better to feel remorse for sins before God than to be able to define the dogma of the Trinity. For 'all is vanity except to love God and serve him only'. There is a certain anti-intellectualism in the contents which was necessary at the time Thomas wrote and which reflects the dominance of scholastic theology at that time; it seemed to have nothing to offer to the needs of the human heart.

Both to meditate upon and to take up the Cross are important: 'In the Cross is salvation, in the Cross is life; in the Cross is protection against our enemies; in the Cross is infusion of heavenly sweetness; in the Cross is strength of mind; in the Cross is joy of spirit; in the Cross is the height of virtue and in the Cross is perfection of holiness. There is no salvation of the soul, nor hope of everlasting life, but in the Cross.' (See his *Prayers and Meditations* on the life and especially the passion of Christ p. 181.)

87

Prayers and Meditations

THOMAS À KEMPIS
(c. 1380–1471)

To imitate Christ it is first necessary, Thomas insisted, that a person prayerfully meditates upon the contents of the four Gospels: and since the larger part of the contents is the account of Holy Week, the passion and death of Jesus, meditating upon Christ means meditating upon his suffering. Yet, since Christ is alive and comes to the humble believer in the Spirit, the meditating is with the living Christ looking back, as it were, on what happened to him previously and what constituted the salvation of the world.

Most of the meditations are in the form of prayers and begin with words such as 'I bless you and give thanks to you, O Lord Jesus Christ . . .' Then there is identification with Christ in considering the events described followed by a request that the meditator will receive an attitude like that displayed by Christ. For example:

I praise and glorify you for your unflinching steadfastness in clinging to the Cross to which you had submitted yourself, and from which no revilings, no specious suggestions, could move you to descend – not even for one short moment would you leave that Cross upon which, of your own free will, you had been raised on high. It was your will there to abide to the end, where of your exceeding love you had placed yourself; there to remain and to die, and there to consummate, in a way fitted to accomplish your purpose, the work which for our sakes you had begun. Grant that I may ever be patient in adversity, and may not fear the taunts of men, nor seek to win their praise; that I may turn away my eyes from the things of this life, and may look for all my comfort to you, my only Saviour. Amen.

Here is the desire to imitate Christ, the Christ who is known through the sacred text of Scripture.

There are a few meditations upon the birth of Jesus and his ministry as well as a few on the resurrection appearances and the ascension into heaven. The majority, however, are on the content of Holy Week and cover all aspects of the Gospel accounts from Palm Sunday to Easter morning. Accepting that we are redeemed in and by the blood of Christ, Thomas looks to Jesus in order to follow, imitate and love him. 'O most adorable Jesus, brightest mirror of a holy life, grant your unworthy servant so to meditate upon your most sweet and perfect example, that I may be led to fashion all my actions and behaviour in accordance with it; that I may learn to be meek and lowly in heart . . . watchful in temptation, patient under correction, prompt in obedience . . .'

I have produced a modern edition under the title *Christ for all Seasons* (Marshall Pickering), which is slightly shorter than the older English translations of the Latin original, *Meditationes et Orationes*.

88

Centuries of Meditations

THOMAS TRAHERNE
(1637–1674)

Traherne's short life included study at Oxford, ordination into the Church of England, incumbency at Credenhill, near Hereford and the office of priest or chaplain in or near London. This book existed from the 1660s only as a manuscript until 1908, five years after the first publication of his poems by Bertram Dobell. The spirituality is that of a man who loves nature, and sees God's glory both transcending it and yet in and through it; who believes that the human soul is the place where God wants to dwell and who sees in Christ the full revelation and salvation of God. There are four sets of one hundred meditations, of varying length but mostly short.

Here are some examples of his thought and style. First, on enjoying the world:

To contemn the world and to enjoy the world are things contrary to each other. How then can we contemn the world, which we are born to enjoy? Truly there are two worlds. One was made by God, the other by men. That made by God was great and beautiful. Before the Fall it was Adam's joy and the Temple of his glory. That made by men is a Babel of confusions: invented riches, pomps and vanities, brought in by sin. Give all (saith Thomas à Kempis) for all. Leave the one that you may enjoy the other.

Secondly, on the actual practice of meditation:

> What is more easy and sweet than meditation? Yet in this hath God commended his love that by meditation it is to be enjoyed. As nothing is easier than to think, so nothing is more difficult than to think well. The easiness of thinking we received from God, the difficulty of thinking well proceeded from ourselves. Yet in truth, it is far more easy to think well than ill, because good thoughts be sweet and delightful: evil thoughts are full of discontent and trouble. So that an evil habit and custom have made it difficult to think well, not Nature. For by nature nothing is so difficult as to think amiss.

Thirdly on love in the soul:

> Whether it be the soul itself, or God in the soul, that shines by love, or both, it is difficult to tell: but certainly the love of the soul is the sweetest thing in the world. I have often admired what should make it so excellent. If it be God that loves, it is the shining of his essence; if it be the soul, it is God's image; it is be both it is a double benefit.

The *Meditations* reveal to us a man who rediscovered 'felicity' in his adult life and regarded it as akin to the untarnished goodness of the little child. It is this which he communicates and which gives an air of excitement to the reading of his *Meditations*.

89

How I became a Christian

KANZO UCHIMURA
(1861–1930)

The first son of a samurai (warrior-knight) he became a
Christian while studying at Sapporo Agricultural College in
Japan. With fellow students he founded in 1881 a non-Western
version of Christianity which is known as *mukyokai* – the non-
church (i.e. non Western) movement – which still exists. It
has its major following amongst the educated classes, especially
academics and students. The story of how he came to faith in
Jesus Christ from traditional Japanese religion is told by him
in *How I became a Christian: out of my Diary*, which was translated
into most of the northern European languages in the 1890s.
His twenty-two volume commentary on the Bible testifies to
his love of and careful reading and study of the Bible.

In the Introduction to this story of his conversion, the
founding of the *mukyokai*, his visit to America and his studies
there, as well as his evaluation of Christianity, he wrote:

I propose to write how I became a Christian and not why.
The so-called 'philosophy on conversion' is not my theme.
I will only describe its 'phenomena' and will furnish material
for more disciplined minds than mine to philosophize upon.
I early contracted the habit of keeping my diary, in which
I noted down whatever ideas and events that came to pass
upon me. I made myself a subject of careful investigation,
and found it more mysterious than anything I ever have

studied. I jotted down its rise and progress, its falls and backslidings, its joys and hopes, its sins and darkness; and notwithstanding all the awfulness that attends such an observation like this, I found it more seriously interesting than any study I had ever undertaken. I call my diary a 'log book' as a book in which is entered the daily progress of this poor bark towards the upper haven through sins, and tears and many a woe. I might just as well call it a 'biologist's sketch book' in which is kept the accounts of all the morphological and physiological changes of a soul in its embryological development from a seed to a full-eared corn.

He tells of how 'Christian monotheism laid its axe at the root of all my superstitions. All the vows I had made, and the manifold forms of worship with which I had been attempting to appease my angry gods could now be dispensed with by owning this one God and my reason and my conscience responded "Yes"!'

Because of the samurai background, in which to be a 'priest' is considered an 'inferior' and 'sentimental' way of life, he had many battles to overcome within himself before he could even study theology seriously and give himself to the calling of Christian preacher and teacher. This book is a sound account of what conversion and commitment to Christ meant in Japan nearly a century ago.

90

The Spiritual Life

EVELYN UNDERHILL
(1875 – 1941)

After a religious conversion in 1907, Miss Underhill turned to the study of the Christian mystics and eventually produced a book, *Mysticism: a study in the nature and development of man's spiritual consciousness* (1st edn 1911; 13th edn 1940). She translated various books on mystical theology and spirituality and wrote other works on this topic. Apart from her academic work as translator and editor she was also a spiritual director and a conductor of retreats. Some of her addresses at these retreats were published. She also produced an important book entitled *Worship* (1936).

In 1936 she gave four talks on BBC radio about the spiritual life: these were published soon afterwards in a revised and expanded form. She explained: 'My object was to present some of the great truths concerning man's spiritual life in simple language; treating it, not as an intense form of other-worldliness remote from the common ways and incompatible with the common life, but rather as the heart of all real religion and therefore of vital concern to ordinary men and women.' It may be claimed that she put into these talks, and into the subsequent book, the fruits of her knowledge and experience of spirituality for the last forty years.

She insisted that 'a spiritual life is simply a life in which all that we do comes from the centre, where we are anchored in God: a life soaked through and through by a sense of his reality

and claim, and self-given to the great movement of his will.'
It was her belief that most of our conflicts and difficulties come
from trying to deal with the spiritual and practical aspects of
our life separately instead of realising them as parts of one
whole.

At times she is quite blunt. For example:

Many people suggest by their behaviour that God is of far
less importance than their bath, morning paper or early cup
of tea. The life of co-operation with God must begin with
a full and practical acceptance of the truth that God alone
matters; and that he, the Perfect, always desires perfection.
Then it will inevitably press us to begin working for
perfection; first in our own characters and actions, next in
our homes, surroundings, profession and country . . .

Therefore *The Spiritual Life* is a life for all who will venture forth
to follow Christ Jesus. It is a life in which, in St Augustine's
words, 'God is the only reality, and we are only real in so far
as we are in his order and he in us'. And 'the true source books
of Christian spirituality', she insisted, 'are the Psalter and the
New Testament – but this fact is not always appreciated by
beginners.'

91

A Guide to Prayer

ISAAC WATTS
(1674–1748)

Watts is remembered as the great hymnwriter of the Congregational Church. He rendered the psalms into congregational hymns and also wrote such fine hymns as 'When I survey the wondrous Cross', 'Jesus shall reign', and 'There is a land of pure delight'. In fact there is a good case for describing the collections of his hymns (1709 and 1719) which he saw published as spiritual classics. It was Watts who shaped out the pattern of the congregational hymn as we know it for he was a new kind of ballad-maker. Through his influence and that of the Wesleys hymns became an important part of the basis of expression of spirituality for Christians throughout the world.

However, Watts was also concerned about the place of prayer in congregational worship, where there was no set liturgy. So he wrote *A Guide and Spirit of Prayer* (1715). It was often reprinted and the edition I have came out to commemorate the two hundredth anniversary of his death in 1948.

It is a kind of text-book written with conviction and with a concern that the public prayers offered in worship should be according to the revealed will of God concerning the nature of prayer. Thus he deals with the invocation of God and the adoring, confessing to, petitioning, pleading with, dedicating to, and thanking him. He also looks at the gift of prayer which 'is one of the noblest and most useful in the Christian life and therefore to be sought with earnest desire and diligence'. Here he gives much sound advice on the preparation necessary in order to pray usefully and fruitfully in an extempore way in public. The gift of prayer has to be polished, as it were, in order to function properly for the edification of the people of God.

Of course Watts also sees a very important relationship between the daily prayer-life of the pastor or leader and the quality and spirituality of the prayers offered to God on behalf of the congregation. There is preparation of the heart as well as of the mind for participation in extempore worship. 'Take frequent occasion, in the midst of your duties in the world', he wrote, 'to lift up your heart to God: he is ready to hear a sudden sentence and will answer the breathings of a holy soul towards himself.'

We are living in times when some churches which traditionally have used set liturgies are having occasional services of worship without a set form. Perhaps they, along with those churches which only have extempore worship, will benefit from the study of Watt's little book for its valuable help in the approach to and preparation of prayers. Of course, it makes no reference to the use of charismatic gifts for such use was not contemplated in the eighteenth century.

92

Hymns

CHARLES WESLEY
(1707–1788)

Charles Wesley is generally regarded as the most gifted of English hymnwriters. Certainly he was the most prolific – 7,270 hymns came from his pen, some of which are of the highest quality. The hymns give vibrant expression to the evangelical faith and experience which he, with his brother, John, was commending to the world.

The hymn he wrote to celebrate his conversion opens by asking: 'Where shall my wandering soul begin? How shall I all to heaven aspire?' In the first *Methodist Hymn Book*, edited by John Wesley in 1779, the majority of the hymns are by Charles. They cover the whole range of the themes of Christian worship. One of these themes, and one not always connected with the 'evangelical Wesleys' is that of the Sacrament of the Lord's Supper. In 1745 Charles published *Hymns on the Lord's Supper*; some but not all of these appeared in the first Methodist Hymn Book, as they have also done in subsequent editions of this great book.

Those who read the *Hymns on the Lord's Supper* will be given a first- class introduction to a theology of the sacrament as well as to a practical guide as to how rightly to receive the sacramental body and blood of Jesus Christ. In fact the work of Wesley in this connexion merits the title 'Sacramental' as well as 'Evangelical' to the Revival of the eighteenth century (see the splendid study of the Wesleys by J.E. Rattenbury).

Here is one of the less well-known ones:

> O Thou who this mysterious bread
>   Didst in Emmaus break,
> Return, herewith our souls to feed
>   And to thy followers speak.
>
> Unseal the volume of Thy grace,
>   Apply the gospel word,
> Open our hearts to see Thy face,
>   Our hearts to know the Lord.
>
> Of Thee we commune still, and mourn
>   Till Thou the veil remove;
> Talk with us, and our hearts shall burn
>   With flames of fervent love.
>
> Enkindle now the heavenly zeal
>   And make Thy mercy known,
> And give our pardon'd souls to feel
> That God and love are one.

Better known ones include 'Come, Thou everlasting Spirit, Bring to every thankful mind' and 'Author of Life Divine, Who has a Table spread'.

In his Preface to the *Methodist Hymn Book*, John Wesley explained 'that which is of infinitely more moment than the spirit of poetry is the spirit of piety' which he hoped users would find breathing through the hymns. Then, he added that, 'when Poetry thus keeps its place, as the handmaid of Piety, it shall attain not a poor perishable wreath, but a crown that fadeth not away.' Certainly with Charles Wesley excellent poetry does keep its place as the handmaid of spirituality and for this reason it repays both the reading and the singing!

93

A Plain Account of Christian Perfection

JOHN WESLEY
(1703–1791)

Wesley was a remarkable man who travelled thousands of miles on horseback to preach the Gospel, was a brilliant organiser of human beings, had a gift as a translator of German hymns, edited the works of Christians of a variety of traditions, and wrote sermons and treatises which make for lively and instructive reading today. One of his most important little books is this on the Christian life as the exercise of perfect love. Not only does he set out his teaching on what he saw as the distinctive contribution of the people called Methodists to Christian spirituality, but he also acquaints the reader with aspects of his own spiritual pilgrimage. He insists and maintains that Christian Perfection (maturity in God's love) is the whole point and purpose of the Christian life. Methodism was raised up by God to spread 'scriptural holiness' throughout Britain – and from there throughout the world.

Within his own lifetime the book had gone through six editions and since his death has gone to over thirty more. With his brother Charles (see p. 191) he maintained (i) that Christian Perfection is that love of God and the neighbour which implies deliverance from all sin: (ii) that this is received merely by faith; (iii) that it is given instantaneously in one moment; (iv) that we are to accept it (not at death, but) every moment: that now is the accepted time, now is the day of salvation.

The perfection of which he speaks is not an absolute but a

relative perfection, but he uses the expression because of its roots in the Bible and in Christian tradition. He explained:

I know many that love God with all their heart. He is their one desire, their one delight, and they are continually happy in him. They love their neighbour as themselves. They feel as sincere, fervent, constant a desire for the happiness of every man, good or bad, friend or enemy, as for their own. They rejoice evermore, pray without ceasing, and in everything give thanks. Their souls are continually streaming up to God, in holy joy, prayer and praise . . . But even these souls dwell in a shattered body, and are so pressed down thereby that they cannot always exert themselves as they would by thinking, speaking, and acting precisely right. For want of better bodily organs, they must at times think, speak, or act wrong; not indeed through a defect of love, but through a defect of knowledge. And while this is the case, notwithstanding that defect, and its consequences, they fulfil the law of love. Yet as even in this case, there is not full conformity to the perfect law, so the most perfect do on this very account need the blood of atonement, and may properly for themselves, as well as for their brethren, say: 'Forgive our trespasses'.

Relative perfection, that is, Christian maturity is, however, a very high calling!

94

The Life and Death of the Reverend John Fletcher

JOHN WESLEY
(1703–1791)

John William Fletcher (1729–1785) was Swiss by birth and education. He settled in England, was greatly influenced by the Methodist movement and was ordained a priest of the Church of England in 1757. In 1760 he became Vicar of Madeley in Shropshire where he continued to serve the Methodist movement. In Fletcher Wesley saw the daily reality of Christian perfection, spiritual maturity and scriptural holiness. In fact he designated him as his successor as the leader of Methodism but he died before Wesley. This account by Wesley of the life and death of his friend was based on accounts supplied by Fletcher's widow and brother and is as much a study in personal holiness as a biography. There have been other biographies since Wesley's which give more information about Fletcher and his ministry but this first one is unique in that it is primarily a spiritual study.

Wesley presented this account of Fletcher's communion with God which was described to him by his widow:

Although he enjoyed communion with God, more or less, at all times and in all places, yet I frequently heard him observe that the seasons of his closest communion were always in his own house, or in church; usually in the latter. It is much to be lamented that we have no account of it from his own pen. It was his constant endeavour to maintain an uninterrupted sense of the presence of God. In order to do this, he was slow of speech, and had the greatest government of his words. Indeed, he both acted, and spoke, and thought, as under the eye of God. And thus setting God always before him, he remained unmoved in all occurrences; at all times and on every occasion possessing inward recollection. Nor did I ever see him diverted therefrom on any occasion whatever, either going out or coming in, whether by ourselves or in company. Sometimes he took his journeys alone; but above a thousand miles I have travelled with him; during which neither change of company, place, nor the variety of circumstances which naturally occur in travelling ever seemed to make the least difference in this firm attention to the presence of God . . . He was always striving to raise his own and every other spirit to a close and immediate communion with God. And I can say with truth, all his union with me was so intermingled with prayer and praise that every employment and every meal was, as it were, perfumed therewith.

There were many testimonies from others to bear out the truth of what she described. 'Grace was in all his steps, heaven in his eye and in all his gestures were sanctity and love.'

Wesley's account of Fletcher's life and death is, perhaps, to Methodism and Evangelical Religion, what Athanasius' account of Antony's life and death is to Greek Orthodoxy and monasticism.

95

Forty-four Sermons

JOHN WESLEY
(1703–1791)

These sermons have a special place in Methodism. Not only do they give a comprehensive insight into the teaching on faith, morality and spirituality provided by Wesley but they also are part of the doctrinal foundation of Methodism. For decades Methodist local preachers have been required to read these sermons and be tested on their knowledge of them before they were fully accredited as preachers on the circuit of chapels. As first published in four volumes (1746; 1748; 1750 and 1760) they are not verbatim records of what Wesley preached but rather the substance of sermons to which he added illustrations, topical references and so on. No doubt each of them was preached in one form or another in a variety of places as Wesley went from place to place on horseback preaching, teaching and organising.

Wesley claimed in the preface: 'I desire plain truth for plain people: therefore, of set purpose, I abstain from nice and philosophical speculations; from all perplexed and intricate reasonings . . . I labour to avoid all words which are not easy to be understood, all which are not used in common life . . . I have accordingly set down . . . what I find in the Bible concerning the way to heaven; with a view to distinguish this way of God from all those which are the inventions of men. I have endeavoured to describe the true, the scriptural, experimental (that is based on experience) religion, so as to omit nothing which is a real part thereof, and to add nothing thereto which is not.' He wished to guard young Christians from the mere practices of religion and help them to have heart-religion, which is faith working by love; to warn those who know this heart-religion of the dangers facing them so that they did not backslide.

The topics covered relate to the central themes of the Gospel, regeneration or the new birth, conversion, repentance and faith, adoption as children of God, the Christian life, enjoying an assurance of salvation, holiness of life, facing temptation and suffering, self-denial, the place of the Law, the character of disciples of the kingdom of heaven, the use of money and the call to perfection of love. Wesley sets such high standards that it has often been said that his description (from Acts 26:2 – 'you almost persuade me') of the 'almost Christian' is in fact, for most pastors or evangelists the description of a normal Christian. Wesley's sermons are for those who wish to be challenged by the high calling of God in Christ Jesus to entire consecration of themselves to his service.

He himself confessed: 'I want to know one thing – the way to heaven; how to land safely on that happy shore. He has written it down in a book. O give me that book! At any price give me the Book of God! I have it: here is knowledge enough for me. Let me be a man of one book . . . In his presence I open, I read his Book . . .' His sermons reflect this commitment to God and his Word. For this, if for no other reason, they are worth reading.

96

The Journals

GEORGE WHITEFIELD
(1714–1770)

Whitefield was the greatest orator and preacher of the eighteenth century. What is less well known is that he was also a saintly man, most lovable and humble. His career as a travelling evangelist in Britain and America was amazing and his Herculean work can only be explained by reference to the presence and power of the Holy Spirit. He was not an organiser like his great contemporary, John Wesley, but he did inspire people to great faith, devotion and vision by his example and message. His *Journals* cover the period of his life from December 1737 when he first sailed from London to Georgia until the spring of 1745. In this period he crossed and recrossed the Atlantic Ocean five times and witnessed spiritual awakening in Britain and America. The *Journals* reveal a young man whose heart is on fire for the Lord, who loves and cares for people, and who is thrilled to be able to preach the Gospel.

At the age of 24 he was preaching to miners near Bristol:

Friday, March 30. Preached this afternoon near Coal-Pit Heath . . . where great numbers of colliers live. I believe there were about two thousand people assembled on this occasion. The weather was exceedingly fair, the hearers behaved very well, and the place where I preached, being near the maypole, I took occasion to warn them of misspending their time in revelling and dancing. Oh, that all such entertainments were put a stop to. I see no other way to effect it, but by going boldly, and calling people from such lying vanities in the Name of Jesus Christ. The reformation which is brought about by a coercive power, will be only outward and superficial: but that which is done by the force of God's Word, will be inward and lasting. Lord make me meet by thy grace for such work, and then send me.

Preaching was central to his life but Whitefield also was active in raising money for charity schools in England and for an orphanage in Georgia. Here is what he wrote at Savannah, when he was only 25:

Tuesday, March 25. Went to Bethesda, and, with full assurance of faith, laid the first brick of the great house. The workmen attended, and with me kneeled down and prayed. After we had sung a hymn, I gave a word of exhortation to the labourers, and bid them remember to work heartily, knowing that they worked for God. Much satisfaction appeared to be amongst them, and blessed be God's holy name. His work prospers much in our hands. Nearly twenty acres of land are cleared and almost ready for planting. Two houses are raised, and one nearly finished. All the timber of the great house is sawn . . . a good part of the foundation is dug and many thousands of bricks ready for use. Nearly forty children are now under my care and nearly a hundred mouths are daily supplied with food from our store. The expense is great, but our great and good God, I am persuaded, will enable me to defray it . . .'

Read his *Sermons* as you look through the *Journals*.

97

A Practical View

WILLIAM WILBERFORCE
(1759–1833)

Wilberforce is remembered particularly for his work in the abolition of the slave trade. He was born in Hull and was a long-serving Member of Parliament. As an evangelical Christian he belonged to the Clapham Sect, a group who were involved in public life and who sought to evangelise those who had money and property. To them he addressed his *A Practical View of the Prevailing Religious System of Professed Christians in the Higher and Middle Classes of this Country contrasted with Real Christianity* (1787). The book immediately became a bestseller even though it is long. It was not usual for a politician to write such an obviously evangelical and theological book! Through abridged versions, the book has been made more accessible to modern readers in this century.

The topics covered are these: the inadequate conceptions of Christianity held by people in Britain; the state of human nature according to biblical teaching – it is sinful and in need of forgiveness and renewal; how the majority of nominal Christians do not have a true understanding of the Lord Jesus Christ and the Holy Spirit; how practical religion can fail because it is not faith working by love; and advice and hints on how change can occur in the state of religion.

Near the end of the book he addresses those who aspire to have real Christianity:

Let true Christians with suitable earnestness strive to recommend their faith in everything, and to silence the idle gibes of ignorant objectors. Let them vindicate boldly the cause of Christ in an age when so many who bear the name of Christians are ashamed of him. And let them consider that the important duty of halting for a while the fall of their country devolves on them. Perhaps, too, they will perform a still greater service to society, not by interference in politics, but by restoring the influence of religion and of raising the standard of morality.

Let them be active, useful and generous towards others while being moderate and self-denying in themselves. Let them be as ashamed of idleness, as they would be of sin. When providence blesses them with affluence, let them show by their modest demeanour, and by their absence of display that, without appearing odd, they are not slaves of fashion. Rather, they consider it their duty to set an example of moderation and sobriety, and to reserve for nobler and more disinterested purposes the money which others waste in ostentation, dress, carriages and horses. Let them show, in short, moderation in all worldly things as becomes those whose concerns are set on objects higher than any which this world affords, and who possess, within themselves a sufficiency of satisfaction and comfort, which the world looks for in futility and dissipation.

Perhaps there is a message here for affluent Western Christians!

98

The Cloud of Unknowing

AN ANONYMOUS ENGLISH MONK
(c.1380)

Written in the late fourteenth century this book holds an
important place both in Western spirituality and English
literature. It was not intended for beginners in the Christian
life for it takes for granted that its reader will be familiar with
prayer, meditation upon the life and passion of our Lord, and
the effort to live the moral life. Rather it is aimed at those who
feel a deep and mysterious desire to press on in prayer in order
to help them discover whether this desire is truly from God
or is merely human curiosity or affectation. This desire is,
however, not really a desire but '. . . something which you
are at a loss to describe, which moves you to desire what you
know not what.'

The author leads his readers into deep waters as he describes
the nature of genuine contemplation and spiritual union with
God. The route to this goal is the way of negation. First of all
there is a separation from the world and its creatures by leaving
them behind in 'the cloud of forgetting'. This is achieved by
meditating upon the passion of Jesus and upon one's sins.
Beyond 'the cloud of forgetting' is the thicker 'cloud of
unknowing' and it can only be penetrated by 'a sharp dart of
longing love'. Though the mind can help in approaching the
cloud as it holds on to God's gracious promises, only love (the
affective power of the soul) can make the final part of the
journey. This is because God is transcendent and therefore

cannot truly be known by reason; only the power of love can break through the darkness to unite with him.

God fits himself exactly to our souls by adapting his Godhead to them; and our souls are fitted exactly to him by the worthiness of our creation after his image and likeness. He, by himself alone, and no one but he, is fully sufficient, and much more so, to fulfil the will and desire of our souls. And our soul, because of his renewing grace, is wholly enabled to comprehend by love the whole of him who is incomprehensible to every created knowing power; that is, to the souls of angels and of men.

The distinction between the 'loving power' and the 'knowing power' is very important. God is always finally incomprehensible to the latter – the work of the intellect. However, by grace, God is genuinely comprehensible by love: and the comprehension of God in love is everlasting bliss. In contemplation love pierces the cloud of unknowing to experience 'the wonderful miracle of love' – union with God.

This book begins with an invocation of the Holy Trinity and takes for granted that union with God is union with the Holy Trinity of Love. However, it is for mature Christians only; and it is for those who, being mature and having consulted a spiritual director, feel drawn towards the practice of contemplative prayer.

99

Theologia Germanica

AN ANONYMOUS AUTHOR
(c.1350)

In 1516 Martin Luther, not yet a reformer of the Church but
a professor of theology in search of God and truth, published
a little book at Wittenberg. It had neither title nor author and
so he provided it with the following heading: 'A spiritual, noble
little book. Of right discrimination and reason. What the old
man is and what the new. What is Adam's and what is God's,
and how Adam shall die and Christ arise.' He republished it
again, twice in 1518. Soon it gained its present title, *Theologia
Germanica*.

At this stage in the development of the German
Reformation it contained what Luther and men of kindred
spirit needed to hear – a warm, lively piety, and theology
for the sake of holiness and communion with God. Later,
when the book was attracting the interest of the radical
reformers, the Anabaptists, Luther showed less interest in
it. However, there were always those in the German Lutheran
Church who valued it, especially those who came to be called
the Pietists. Later it was welcomed and widely read in Britain
through the appearance of the English translation by Susanna
Winckworth in 1874. Once more it is attracting attention in
the English-speaking world.

It teaches that God draws men to himself through the
threefold way of purification, enlightening and union. Here
the book repeats traditional teaching:

Now be assured that no one can be united with God unless he has first been enlightened. And so there are three ways. First, purification; secondly, enlightening; thirdly, union. Purification belongs to such as are beginning and repenting, and takes place in three ways: by contrition and sorrow for sin, by full and free confession, by perfect penitence. Enlightening belongs to such as are growing, and likewise takes place in three ways – by the rejection of sin, by the practice of virtue and good works, and by the willing endurance of adversity and tribulations. Union belongs to such as are perfect, and is also brought to pass in three ways – by pureness and singleness of heart, by godly love and by the contemplation of God, the Creator of all things.

Thus the goal is the contemplating, loving and adoring of God and the enjoyment of communion with him.

This mystical quest is centred on Jesus Christ, the new Adam, for he is the Son of God who became man so that sinners through him might be truly renewed in God's image. In this saving activity the human self has to be wholly surrendered to God and set free of self- trust in order to have genuine faith in God. The book ends with a prayer 'that we may deny and renounce ourselves, and forsake all things through God, and die to our own self-will, and live unto God alone and to Christ's will.'

100

The Way of a Pilgrim

AN ANONYMOUS RUSSIAN WRITER

The widespread use of the Jesus Prayer ('Lord Jesus Christ, Son of God, have mercy upon me, a sinner') in English-speaking Christianity owes its origins – more than anything else – to the reading of this little book, which was first translated into English by E.M French in 1943. Since then there have been other translations and various editions. A sequel, *The Pilgrim continues his way*, has been translated. However, it is the first which by its simplicity ranks as a Christian classic.

The pilgrim of the title is a Russian Christian in the second half of the nineteenth century. The story, told by himself, begins as he goes to the Liturgy in church and hears the command, 'Pray constantly' (1 Thess 5:17). This sets him off on a voyage of enquiry and discovery. He visits holy men in monasteries until eventually he receives this advice in a cell of a monk:

The ceaseless Jesus Prayer is a continuous, uninterrupted call on the holy name of Jesus Christ with the lips, mind, and heart; and in the awareness of his abiding presence it is a plea for his blessing in all undertakings, in all places, at all times, even in sleep. The words of the Prayer are: 'Lord Jesus Christ, have mercy on me!' Anyone who becomes accustomed to this Prayer will experience great comfort as well as the need to say it continuously. He will become accustomed to it to such a degree that he will not be able to do without it and eventually the Prayer will of itself flow in him.

The monk then introduced him to the collection of writings of Greek Orthodox spirituality known as the *Philokalia* (see p. 129) commenting that 'this book contains complete and detailed instructions about ceaseless prayer'. He added that its great value is that it contains a clear explanation of the ideas that are mysteriously presented in the Bible.

Thus the pilgrim began to use the Jesus Prayer and after some time he was able to say: 'Now I walk and say the Jesus Prayer without ceasing and it is more precious to me than anything else in the world . . . When the cold air chills me, I begin saying the Prayer with greater intensity and I warm up. When hunger begins to overcome me I begin saying the name of Jesus Christ more frequently and I forget I wanted to eat. When I become sick and feel rheumatic pain in my back and legs I pay greater attention to the Prayer and I do not feel pain. When someone offends me I remember how sweet the Jesus Prayer is and I forget everything, walk in a semi-conscious state without worries, interests or temptations . . .' This is but the beginning for there is the advanced stage when the Prayer is the source of ceaseless self-activating prayer of and in the heart. The pilgrimage is therefore a real, physical visiting of places and meeting people and serving the Lord on the way; it is also a deepening use of the Prayer until the Prayer is truly lodged in the heart and there, as it were, creates communion with God.

Epilogue

How can one bring to an end this introduction to one hundred special books, written by over ninety holy people? There is no adequate or even satisfactory way of doing it; but what I shall do is to offer three qualities or notes of the Christian life to which each book, in its own individual, even sometimes idiosyncratic, way points.

First of all the true Christian is a person with tremendous zest and concentration gained in the contemplating of God and channelled into the loving of God, and the doing of his will. In fact this love is not that person's own but is the love of God given in and through Jesus by the Holy Spirit. Being in love with God, the saint is ready to do such things as others, especially nominal Christians, would describe as ridiculous or mad. So the first quality or note is INTENSITY.

In the second place, the true Christian sees life not as restricted by 'three score years and ten' but as opening up under and in God not only into infinity and eternity but also into richness of glory. Further, she or he belongs not merely to a little group here or there but to a great crowd of witnesses who exist through the centuries and into that heavenly throng who worship the Lord in the beauty of holiness. So the second quality or note is VASTNESS.

Finally, the true Christian begins to enjoy God in this life and this enjoyment is ever set to become deeper and more fulfilling. The gift of God to the believer is eternal life and those whom God calls to himself he calls permanently. His love when bestowed is an everlasting love. So the third quality or note is PERMANENCE.

Intensity, vastness, permanence – total and complete and

utter satisfaction; these are the qualities or notes of the life to which God the Father calls us through the Lord Jesus and by the Holy Spirit. This is the life to which these classics both witness and urge us to experience for the glory of God and our own perfection and fulfilment.

To be 'a man of one Book' – the Bible – may mean for many of us being also those who are guided by the saints to the one Book and its message of the intensity, vastness and permanence of the love of God in Jesus Christ our Lord.